THE MODERN MARKETING ARSENAL

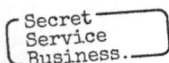

Secret
Service
Business.

https://secretservice.biz
Secret Service Business Pty Ltd (publisher)
de Lacy, Laura (author)
Secret Service Business Series, Book Three
The Modern Marketing Arsenal: Ways & Means to Promote a Small Skill-or-Service Business (& Which to Choose to Get the Most Bang for Your Marketing Buck)
ISBN Paperback: 978-0-6450683-4-4
ISBN eBook: 978-0-6450683-5-1
BUSINESS

(*) greenhill

https://greenhillpublishing.com.au/

Typeset Calluna 10/16
Cover Image by Adobe Stock
Editing by Isabelle Russell, New Zealand
Interior illustrations by
Tatsiana Teush, Poland
Cover and book design by
Green Hill Publishing

The material in this publication is of the nature of general comment only, and does not represent professional advice. It is not intended to provide specific guidance for particular circumstances and it should not be relied on as the basis for any decision to take action or not take action on any matter which it covers. Readers should obtain professional advice where appropriate before making any such decision. The author and the publisher make no representations regarding any results that will or may be achieved by relying or acting on the information and, to the maximum extent permitted by law, disclaim all responsibility and liability to any person, arising directly or indirectly from any person taking or not taking action based on the information contained herein.

The author and the publisher have no responsibility for the persistence or accuracy of URLs for external or third-party internet websites referred to in this book, and do not guarantee that any content on such websites is, or will remain, accurate and appropriate. Except where indicated, any trade marks mentioned in this publication are used without permission. The author and the publisher have no association with these trade marks or the trade mark owners. The names of individuals may have been altered for the purpose of protecting their identity.

THE SECRET SERVICE BUSINESS SERIES ❸

THE MODERN MARKETING ARSENAL

Ways & Means to Promote a
Small Skill-or-Service Business
(& Which to Choose to Get the Most
Bang for Your Marketing Buck)

LAURA DE LACY

For the owners of small skill-or-service businesses, ready to scale up but grappling with the perils and possibilities of modern marketing.

READ THIS FIRST

This book is one of three in the *Secret Service Business Series*:
  1. **Secret Service Marketing:** *The Underground Guide to Modern Marketing for Small Skill-or-Service Businesses*
  2. **The Secret Service Website Formula:** *3 Steps to a Lead Machine Website for Small Skill-or-Service Business Owners, their Web Designers & Content Creators*
  3. **The Modern Marketing Arsenal:** *Ways & Means to Promote a Small Skill-or-Service Business (& Which to Choose to Get the Most Bang for Your Marketing Buck)*

To reap the best possible results, reading the books in the above order is recommended. As tempting as it may be to skip ahead, the first two books lay critical foundations to give your marketing tools and activities the best possible chance; reducing the time and money you'll need to spend on them in the future.

Reading *Secret Service Marketing* first is all the more important if you've been struggling to cultivate a winning business concept or convert a worthy concept into a viable business model. Building a website or promoting your offerings without certainty of the value your business provides, clarity on how to package, price and present your services, or without the tools and techniques to convert leads into sales is a surefire way to blow your budget. Take some time to read *Secret Service Marketing* and *The Secret Service Website Formula* before making any major marketing decisions and your business and bank account will thank you for it.

CONTENTS

SECRET SERVICE MARKETING: A RAPID-FIRE RECAP

In the modern world of small business, the ways and means to attract new customers can seem overwhelming and endless. Every day, new business-boosting ideas and opportunities present themselves and, with each one we ignore, many of us feel a pang of guilt that we're not doing as much for our business, or bank account, as we should be.

But the good news is that most of these opportunities are irrelevant. They're geared for goods-based, internet marketing or small businesses generally – not the highly specific needs of SSBs.

As explained in the first book of the *Secret Service Business Series*, a **small skill-or-service business (SSB)** is one that:

Has 0 to 19 employees;

- Draws on a body of skills, knowledge and/or resources in a particular area of expertise to satisfy customer needs or expectations;

- Primarily sells information, advice or assistance, manual
  labour, the use or benefit of physical resources, an
  experience, or a unique, handmade or customised end
  product to customers in its local area.

SSBs are different from other businesses, with distinct marketing and design needs (as you'll know if you've read the first two books). But there's a little more to grasp to be able to determine the marketing and promotional options that are a good fit for your business.

When the mud and murk of irrelevant ideas and opportunities are cleared away, there are a finite number of marketing activities worthy of an SSB owner's consideration, which can be boiled down to just 10 types. These comprise the spokes of the *Secret Service Marketing Wheel* – the model that underpins the Secret Service methodology (introduced and explained in Chapter 3 of *Secret Service Marketing* – the first book of the series), recapped for quick reference below.

Figure 1: The Secret Service Marketing Wheel

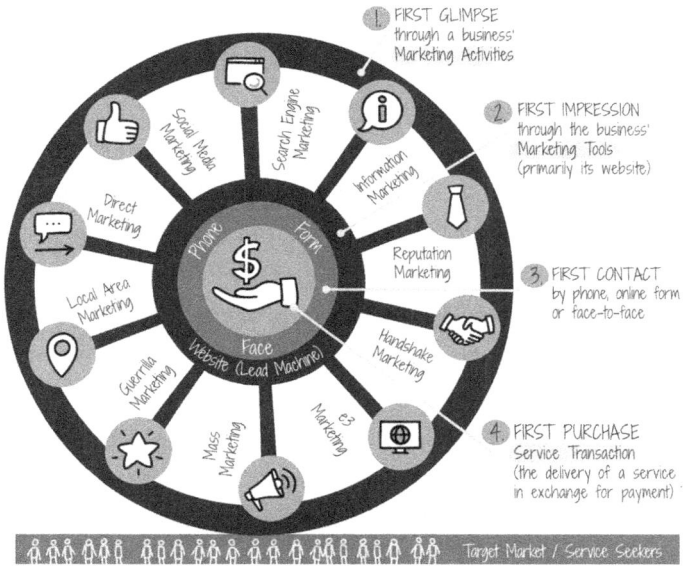

1. FIRST GLIMPSE
   through a business'
   Marketing Activities

2. FIRST IMPRESSION
   through the business'
   Marketing Tools
   (primarily its website)

3. FIRST CONTACT
   by phone, online form
   or face-to-face

4. FIRST PURCHASE
   Service Transaction
   (the delivery of a service
   in exchange for payment)

Social Media Marketing
Search Engine Marketing
Information Marketing
Direct Marketing
Reputation Marketing
Local Area Marketing
Handshake Marketing
Guerrilla Marketing
e3 Marketing
Mass Marketing
Phone
Form
Face
Website (Lead Machine)

Target Market / Service Seekers

The Secret Service Marketing Wheel presents the marketing activities available for SSBs to attract the attention of those seeking out a skill-or-service business – referred to from here as **service seekers** – along with the fundamental tools and steps required to convert them into paying customers. The Wheel is designed to help SSB owners make smarter marketing decisions; decisions that have the capacity to boost business momentum with little to no increase in marketing expenditure.

How the Wheel Works

With the Secret Service approach to marketing, service seekers are funnelled through a series of 'firsts', from unidentified members of a target market through to paying customers. The spokes of *marketing activity* generate awareness of, and interest in, the business' offering – giving service seekers a *first glimpse* of a possible solution. These activities drive traffic to a *website*, which has the pivotal role of connecting with, convincing and converting potential customers into leads through the creation of a favourable *first impression*. From there, leads flow in via website enquiry *form submissions, phone calls* and *face-to-face walk-in enquiries*. This is the all-important *first contact*, which – if handled well and followed up appropriately – can culminate in a *service transaction* or *first purchase*.

Finding the optimum combination of spokes (marketing activities) to connect the rim (our target market) to the hub (our marketing tools and business processes) is how the Marketing Wheel gets and holds momentum, but that doesn't make the spokes the top priority. While marketing activities comprise the largest, most visible area of the Wheel, marketing activity alone is not enough to build a viable, profitable business.

Supporting the Spokes: The Importance of a Strong Hub & Rim

No matter the strength of its spokes, if the hub or rim of a wheel is weak or off-kilter, the vehicle will become increasingly uncomfortable for the operator, or buckle when required to bear weight. The same holds true for marketing an SSB.

The hub is the 'business end' of spokes in a wheel or marketing activities in a business. Just as a hub gives a wheel the capacity to move in a coordinated way via an axle, the hub of the Marketing Wheel (consisting of our marketing tools and business processes) gives our business the capacity to function. If our hub isn't solid enough to support the spokes of marketing activity funnelling customers to it, the business won't get far. Sooner or later it will collapse under the pressure of any remotely effective activity.

At the other end of the spoke is the rim – an equally important consideration for a wheel (or business) to work. The rim supports the spokes at the 'pointy end' of marketing, where our marketing activities make contact with our target market and the rubber of any fancy advertising hits the road. If our target market is poorly defined and the needs of service seekers are overlooked or misunderstood, no amount of marketing activity will help. The spokes won't connect. They'll come jutting out sideways, poking us repeatedly in the hip pocket, with nothing to show for our fancy advertising but big, black burnout marks on our bank statement.

There is more to marketing than marketing activity – just as there is more to a wheel than its spokes – but we've been conditioned to think they're one and the same. Many of us assume that the only way to overcome our marketing struggles is to invest in expensive marketing activity and a new logo to boot. Not only does this mindset have the exact opposite effect – exacerbating the struggle rather than helping us to overcome it – it blocks us from identifying the real root of the problem... the flimsiness of our Marketing Wheel's hub and rim.

The first two books in the *Secret Service Business Series*

provide a framework for overcoming the debilitating effects of this flimsiness.

Book one, *Secret Service Marketing*, strips back the layers of ingrained beliefs and marketing misconceptions that hold so many SSB owners back, replacing them with a mindset and methodology capable of revolutionising the performance of a struggling SSB. It contains practical steps, tools and insights, along with carefully crafted Recovery Missions, to generate maximum impact and lasting change on a tight budget.

The second book, *The Secret Service Website Formula*, provides the blueprints for the development of a **Lead Machine** – a website geared to drive leads to an SSB. As the Marketing Wheel shows, a website is *not* one of the 10 types of marketing activity available to SSBs. It is an essential marketing tool that plays a critical role at the hub of a business' marketing efforts. A website provides the main means for service seekers to research and connect with us once they've been receptive and responsive to our marketing activity. Converting a decent percentage of these service seekers into leads takes more than a stock standard, professional looking website or dumb luck. It takes a website equipped to serve as a Lead Machine, strategically designed to connect, convince and convert. *The Secret Service Website Formula* contains the insights and instructions to create just that, in an easy-to-follow format, suitable for DIYers to experienced, commercial website developers – anyone with a vested interest in creating SSB websites that work.

The book you're reading, *The Modern Marketing Arsenal*, is the third book in the *Secret Service Business Series*. It's been carefully crafted to help you cut through the clutter of options available to reach and attract new customers – presenting only the most applicable and concentrating on those that offer the most bang for an SSB owner's marketing buck.

While *The Modern Marketing Arsenal* can be read on its own or before the others in the series, be aware that – without the insights and outcomes of the first two books – it'll make you no less susceptible to the pitfalls of a weak Marketing Wheel. Reading and implementing each of the three books in order will take more time upfront; however, it'll save an enormous amount of time, effort, money and frustration in the long run. When you feel confident that the hub and rim of your Wheel is strong, use this book to go for broke on the spokes – selecting marketing activities that help you get traction, generate momentum and enjoy a smoother, swifter, more satisfying business ride.

CHAPTER 1.

THE ACTIVITY ARSENAL

*** WARNING! RECAPPED CONTENT AHEAD ***
If you've read Chapter 16 of *Secret Service Marketing*, the content of this chapter will be familiar. Skim down to the *Marketing Activity Quick Reference Guide* and read from there.

Most SSB owners have a preconceived idea about what marketing activity should look like and how much it should cost as a percentage of revenue. But such rigid business beliefs no longer serve us. The game of marketing has changed – *in our favour*. We have more power than we ever dreamed possible, but putting it into play takes awareness and practice. Only by recognising the opportunities available to us and making tactical moves can we access our share of the spoils.

Modern marketing requires a carefully considered gameplan. Observing and imitating the manoeuvres made by big businesses is no longer the smartest play. SSBs are not big businesses – nor are the majority ever intended to be. Seeking to play the game like the big boys on the business field is a surefire way to lose. To win, we need an entirely different approach and attitude; embracing our small size and limited resources as opportunities, not blaming them for our lack of business traction to date.

Building a thriving SSB with next to no ongoing marketing costs is no longer a pipedream. With a Secret Service mindset, a strong business model, a Lead Machine website and a carefully selected suite of marketing activities, we can kick more goals than we ever thought possible.

In order to select the right marketing activities, we first need to know what opportunities are available to us and how to choose between them. We'll explore the individual activities and the prioritisation and selection of these activities shortly but in the meantime, let's shine a light on the arsenal of options at our disposal – the 10 broad types of marketing activity available to SSBs (aka the 10 spokes of the Marketing Wheel).

1. Handshake Marketing

It's only fitting to kick things off with the oldest marketing activity in human history and, arguably, the most crucial to SSB survival. *Handshake marketing* is any marketing activity that involves the development and nourishment of business relationships through one-on-one interaction and connection. It has existed for thousands of years and is as relevant now as it ever was – in the form of *networking, manual sales prospecting, alliance building* and exhibiting at *expos or trade shows*.

2. e3 Marketing

From the oldest form of marketing to one of the newest... *e3 marketing* is a means of generating traffic, leads or sales, through an electronic (e), third party (3) website service. These third party sites exist to serve as intermediaries between buyers and sellers in specific industries or markets. They range from broad marketplaces, like Gumtree, to niche comparator websites such as 'Compare the Market' for insurance. Each e3 site serves as a conduit between buyers and sellers, bringing them together via an online hub. Ideally, the site's brand awareness, buyer database and resources generate a flow of traffic, leads or sales for sellers. The e3 marketing platforms of most relevance to SSBs are *online directories, comparator websites* and *group buying ('daily deal') sites*.

3. Reputation Marketing

Reputation marketing is an ongoing activity aimed to build and preserve a business' public image. At the core of reputation marketing is the familiar concept of *word of mouth.* Word of mouth occurs when customers are so satisfied (or dissatisfied) with our service that they recommend (or disparage) us to their friends, family, associates, or even strangers. Positive word of mouth can be encouraged but it can't be commanded or controlled. To a large extent, it is what it is. However, what we *can* do is capitalise on it (and

any other positive events and occurrences) through two free activities: *online review management* and *public relations (PR) management*.

4. Information Marketing

Information marketing is the sharing of rich, valuable information with an online or offline audience – informing, educating and/or empowering them to become more capable or successful in some way. Empowering your audience to undertake a project or achieve a certain outcome for themselves might sound counterintuitive – on par with revealing the ingredients in a secret sauce. But, in actuality, spilling a few beans can prove incredibly lucrative and generate far more momentum than spilling none at all. The information marketing activities of most relevance to SSBs include *content marketing, group training* and the development and dissemination of *information products*.

5. Search Engine Marketing

Search engine marketing makes the most of search engines (Google, Bing, DuckDuckGo and others) to help businesses get found by internet users who are actively searching for goods, services or solutions online. There are two modes of search engine marketing: *search engine optimisation (SEO)*, which seeks to

help a business' website rank higher in the natural or 'organic' list of search results displayed for relevant search terms, and **search engine advertising (SEA),** which generates exposure through paid advertising.

6. Social Media Marketing

The term social media refers to online platforms (sites and applications) that allow users to create and share content with a pool of friends or followers, for the purposes of social connection and amusement. Popular social networks include Facebook, Instagram, YouTube, LinkedIn, TikTok, X (formerly Twitter) and Pinterest. **Social media marketing** uses one or more of these platforms to reach and engage with a targeted audience. As with search engine marketing, there are two ways to make a business visible to users on social media: the free way, **social media activity** and the paid way, **social media advertising**.

7. Direct Marketing

Direct marketing involves communicating with potential or past customers and contacts via a one-to-one medium of communication – email, phone or mail. The boundaries of direct marketing have been blurred over the years, however the most practical way to define it is a marketing activity that: 1) requires a database or list of individual contact details to initiate,

or 2) is triggered by an individual taking a certain technological action (such as subscribing to a mailing list or phoning a business to make an enquiry). As such, direct marketing encompasses the activities of *telemarketing, email marketing, mobile marketing* and *snail mail marketing*.

8. Local Area Marketing

Local area marketing refers to activities geared to capture the attention and interest of offline buyers within a localised geographic area. This includes *point of sale (POS) promotion, asset advertising, community facility advertising, resident distribution advertising* and *local markets*. The majority of these activities are best suited to businesses that are operationally confined to a particular region due to the delivery of in-person or on-site services (e.g. beauty salons, cafés and trade services).

9. Guerrilla Marketing

Guerrilla marketing is a means of generating public attention and interest by thinking outside the marketing box. It's about creating opportunities to stand out from the crowd; initiating – or capitalising on – events and occurrences that are impressive, memorable and unique. For SSBs, these opportunities tend to fall into three categories: *celebrity appeal marketing, viral marketing* and *street marketing*.

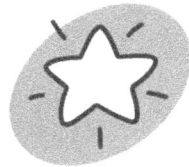

10. Mass Marketing

Mass marketing encompasses activities geared to push an advertising message out to the general public via traditional advertising mediums – mainstream television, radio, print and/or outdoor advertising (billboards, ambient media etc) – referred to collectively as ***mainstream media advertising***. The aim of mass marketing is to generate awareness, interest and desire for a product or service, en masse. While it's one of the most expensive forms of marketing activity, the shift away from it (to online modes of marketing) has rendered some mainstream advertising opportunities more accessible to SSBs than ever before. As such, it's still worth considering.

_____

Activities Explained

A Secret Service Marketer's arsenal is made up of the marketing activities that fall into these 10 categories, plus six marketing *tools* (which we'll set aside for now and return to in Chapter 6). Put simply, marketing activities are ways and means an SSB owner can reach out to a target market to attract the attention of potential customers. For quick reference, these are summarised in the table below.

Figure 2: Secret Service Marketing Activities – A quick reference list

Marketing Type	Marketing Activity (Opportunity)
Handshake Marketing	• Networking • Manual Sales Prospecting • Alliance Building • Expos and Trade Shows
e3 Marketing	• Online Directories • Comparator Websites • Group Buying (Daily Deal) Website Campaigns
Reputation Marketing	• Word of Mouth • Online Review Management • Public Relations Management
Information Marketing	• Group Training • Content Marketing • Information Products
Search Engine Marketing	• Search Engine Optimisation • Search Engine Advertising
Social Media Marketing	• Social Media Activity • Social Media Advertising
Direct Marketing	• Telemarketing • Email Marketing • Mobile Marketing • Snail Mail Marketing
Local Area Marketing	• Point of Sale Promotion • Asset Advertising • Community Facility Advertising • Resident Distribution Advertising • Local Markets
Guerrilla Marketing	• Celebrity Appeal Marketing • Viral Marketing • Street Marketing
Mass Marketing	• Mainstream Media Advertising

To be clear, no business needs all marketing activities. You'd be silly (and broke) if you tried. Instead, the aim of the game is to find the best mix to sustain or grow your business without breaking the bank. This optimum arsenal of activities is different for every business. For some SSBs with a strong business model, it can comprise little more than a few free activities. For others, more trial and error, time, money and business model refinement is required to strike the right balance. There is no 'one size fits all' mix of marketing activities, only one tailored to fit the needs, objectives and resources of a particular business and, importantly, the capabilities and personality of its owner.

Where to Begin

Delving into each marketing activity in the above-listed order might be logical, but it wouldn't be too practical. That's because all marketing activities are not created equal. Some are essential while others are entirely optional. Some are free, requiring little time or money to implement, while others can quickly blow your budget. As Secret Service Marketers, we need to know the difference and act accordingly – prioritising essential, low-cost activities first, and optional, expensive activities last. Luckily for us, some of the most powerful marketing activities for SSBs are freely available to any business owner with the initiative to embrace and action them... so let's start there.

CHAPTER 2.

ACTIVITIES FOR SSB SURVIVAL

Certain marketing activities are part and parcel of building an SSB – they are fundamental to SSB survival, no matter what combination of other activities we employ. These are the ones involving basic human interaction.

As SSB owners, our ability to connect, communicate and serve others is not only at the core of what we do operationally, it's at the core of our marketing efforts. Unlike goods-based businesses, it's virtually impossible for an SSB to survive without some form of real-time human interaction with potential customers.

These essential, interaction-based activities are listed in the right-hand column below, then introduced and explained one-by-one.

Figure 3: Survival Activities

Marketing Type	Marketing Activity (Opportunity)
Handshake Marketing	• Networking • Manual Sales Prospecting
Reputation Marketing	• Word of Mouth
Direct Marketing	• Telemarketing – Inbound
Local Area Marketing	• Point of Sale Promotion – Personal Selling

Networking

Networking is essentially socialising with a view to creating business contacts. The aim is to proactively build a network of connections with like-minded individuals; those who share an interest in our services, industry or target market, or in business and entrepreneurship generally.

Networking usually occurs face-to-face but can be initiated through other mediums. It can take place:

- at formal networking events
- at seminars and workshops
- at business and product launches
- through social media
- by phone
- by email
- anywhere – on a plane, at a BBQ or even in the supermarket.

No matter how a connection is initiated, it's important to understand that one isolated conversation or communication does not build a viable, trust-based business relationship. A proactive investment of time and energy is usually required to develop a connection over time – with face-to-face interactions where possible – to develop trust and an emotional bond.

Successful networkers approach networking as a mutual exchange of interest and energy. They are highly attentive – listening carefully to identify areas of common ground and to support or add value to the other person; looking for opportunities to *give* as well as to *receive*.

When networking, our ability to create quality contacts lies in our intention – to connect with others, or to sell to them. Imagine you're attending a local networking event. You head to the drinks table and get chatting to someone named Jenny about the wine. You ask what she does, which leads to a lengthy conversation about your respective businesses and the discovery that you have similar target markets and challenges. You exchange business cards and Jenny suggests a coffee catch-up later in the week to explore opportunities and support each other's businesses moving forward. You enthusiastically accept and Jenny heads off for a top-up. Meanwhile, seeing you standing alone, Jim pounces. He thrusts a business card under your nose and launches into a rehearsed elevator pitch. You feel awkward and imposed upon, politely taking the card while secretly plotting your escape.

The difference between Jenny and Jim's approach is their intention. Jenny is attending the event with the intention of forming friendships with like-minded local business owners. She is choosing to give her time and energy to other individuals at the event with no expectation of return. She has faith that if she is meant to cross paths with certain people for the benefit of her business, she will – as long as she has the confidence to be herself and initiate follow-up meetings with those she resonates with. This liberates her to be herself.

Jim's intention is different. Fuelled by insecurity, desperation or dollars, he is there to sell. That means he doesn't care who the other attendees are. He views them all the same – as walking, talking dollar signs. Jim attends not with faith but with a fear of missing out on potential sales and not meeting his monthly targets.

Where Jenny's approach *flows*, Jim's is *forced*. She is focused on the *quality* of her contacts, while he is focused on *quantity* – pitching to as many people as possible, before he's earned the trust required to do so.

Pushing an agenda before a foundation of trust is in place, like Jim does, is like picking fruit before it's ripe. It leaves the other person disappointed, with a bitter taste in their mouth. Pushing a self-serving agenda early on, squanders opportunities and stifles relationships. That's not to say we need to wait months or years to sell to or establish a monetary relationship with a new contact. It simply means we need to be guided by them – listening out for their needs and problems and creating an opportunity to explore them further at a suitable time and place (not in the middle of a business breakfast).

In small business, formal and informal networking opportunities arise regularly. It's up to us whether we seize them (attending events and/or striking up conversations with new people) or stifle them (clutching to the individuals with whom we feel comfortable) – bearing in mind that the size and substance of our network is a major determinant of the success of our business.

The more we embrace networking as an essential, ongoing marketing activity, the more opportunities we have to spark lucrative, long-lasting business relationships; a natural byproduct of conscious intention and commitment, human connection and geographic convenience.

Manual Sales Prospecting

Manual sales prospecting utilises basic business tools to mine for sales leads. Just as manual gold prospecting is the act of searching for gold, equipped with only the most basic, manual resources, manual sales prospecting (or prospecting for short) is the act of searching for sales leads. Instead of shovels, screens and sluices, it utilises a database and/or existing network of contacts, a phone, computer and vehicle. It involves keeping an ear out for potential sales opportunities through clients, suppliers and other contacts, then following the bread-crumb trail of actions (connecting with gatekeepers, submitting proposals, etc) to secure viable leads.

Prospecting is an essential marketing activity for most SSBs, however most of us do it in a way that unknowingly contributes to our *Busy/Slow Cycle.*[1] When we're busy with existing work and deadlines, we don't always realise sales are slowing down until an emotional alarm is triggered by an indicative event – such as our bank balance dropping too low or a sudden realisation that there are no new leads in our sales pipeline. Panic kicks in and we hit the phones, mining for work. Inevitably, something comes through – albeit at a heavily discounted price, having quoted out of desperation. We breathe a sigh of relief and the cycle begins again.

Prospecting solely as a means to escape the troughs of a Busy/Slow Cycle may solve a problem in the short-term but creates bigger ones in the long-run. It generates temporary bursts of sales activity which fuel Busy/Slow fluctuations. After each burst of sales, business returns to its natural state which – if no other marketing activities are in place to drive leads – is the *slow* state; a state of inertia.

The key to successful prospecting – reducing the intensity of the Busy/Slow Cycle rather than amplifying it – is to be proactive and consistent, taking action before it becomes necessary. This means actively seeking out sales each and every week, despite a busy schedule. Implementing this change starts by setting a goal, geared to prioritise prospecting as a non-negotiable task in your weekly work schedule.

At first, a prospecting goal should be slightly challenging but easily achievable – just enough to keep sales in your field of vision. Depending on the size and scope of your business, the goal may simply be: 'Spend two hours every Wednesday morning completing four prospecting tasks'. These could include: 1) phoning existing contacts or past clients to scope potential sales opportunities, 2) following up on quotes and enquiries to see if prospects are ready to proceed, 3) phoning or meeting with old/new contacts, or 4) exploring items of industry gossip regarding upcoming projects. Although a few extra phone calls may not sound like much, they can make a world of difference to a business that's spent years at the mercy of the Busy/Slow Cycle.

Word of Mouth

Of all marketing activities, verbal *word of mouth* is one of the most influential. It has the capacity to generate free exposure and scorching hot leads through unsolicited referrals, or to drive service seekers away in droves – quite literally making us or breaking us.

Potential customers are more likely to act on positive word of mouth than marketing or sales communications alone. It's direct and unfiltered, therefore more believable and often far more flattering than anything we could say ourselves. What's more, it induces emotion – a sense of familiarity and trust (connectivity) – which helps to bypass the logic centre in the brain that causes many service seekers to focus heavily on price. Because of this, leads that flow in as a result of word of mouth tend to be easier to convert into sales with less price-based pushback.

Positive word of mouth is crucial for business survival, but what customers say about us (offline, at least) is largely out of our control, creating a bit of a quandary. Of course, we can try offering rewards, gifts or incentives for referring a friend, but for SSBs, structured referral systems tend to fall flat. At the end of the day, we can't hold customers to ransom or demand they promote us to others. That's why, as powerful as it is, it's not wise to rely on verbal word of mouth as a primary marketing activity. It's best viewed as a complementary activity, with any leads that come from it considered a delightfully unexpected bonus.

The best thing we can do to encourage positive word of mouth is to practise continual improvement, professional integrity and high standards. The more we strive for excellence, the more satisfied customers will be – and the more satisfied they are, the more likely they'll be to speak highly of us to others.

Telemarketing – Inbound

Telemarketing gets a pretty bad wrap. Most of us dismiss it as 'cold-calling' but outbound communication (making phone calls) is only one side of the tele-marketing coin, and cold-calling a mere fraction of that. The flipside is *inbound telemarketing* (receiving phone calls), which is just as important as outbound, if not more. How long it takes us to answer our phone, if/when we reply to voice messages plus what we say and how we say it (in both live calls and automated messages) are some of the most crucial but overlooked telemarketing considerations for SSBs. They are a direct reflection of our business' professionalism; providing a strong indication of what doing business with us will be like... light and easy, or a pain in the neck.

All it takes to improve our inbound telemarketing approach and outcomes is to walk through the process of calling our business in the figurative shoes of a potential customer. By consciously reflecting on the experience of those phoning us, we can determine what's undermining it and what's needed – technologically, procedurally or interpersonally – to transform it for the better.

To help with this, a series of questions for consideration are outlined below.

When phone calls are answered...

- How long does the phone usually ring before it's answered?
- Is the phone manner of the person/people answering calls warm, responsive and consistent from one call to the next?
- Are customer enquiries followed up?
- Are commitments made during calls (e.g. promises to email information or phone back later) actioned in a timely manner?
- Do callers ever need to be placed on hold? If yes, what do they hear while on hold (e.g. silence, music or a customised marketing message)?
- With consideration to the above, what systems, procedures and/or staff training could be put in place to improve the experience of calling your business?

When phone calls are not answered...

- Are callers given the opportunity to leave a message via voicemail, answering machine or answering service?
- If so, is the tone of the message warm and welcoming and does it clearly state the name of the business to avoid caller confusion?
- Does the message provide clear instructions for leaving a message and an estimated timeframe for calls to be returned?
- Are calls consistently returned and, if so, how long does it take?
- With consideration to the above, how could the experience of leaving a message be improved?

In an age of online enquiries and instant messaging, those interested enough in our services to make contact by phone are some of the hottest leads we can get. All it takes to capitalise on them is a little awareness, empathy and organisation, along with some readily accessible telephone technology. A few tweaks to your inbound telemarketing processes can go a long way; improving the perception of your business and increasing the number of phone enquiries that convert into sales.

Point of Sale Promotion – Personal Selling

Just as the focus of telemarketing is usually cold-calling, the focus of point of sale (POS) marketing tends to be promotional paraphernalia – posters, table-talkers and other tangible materials designed to catch the attention of customers at a business premises. But POS goes beyond pretty posters. Not only are the intangible aspects of POS promotion far more important, they are applicable to every SSB – whether we serve customers at a business premises or not.

The intangible aspects of POS promotion are the human elements of a sale: the activation of sales systems and procedures, the performance personas of those doing the selling, and the sales skills, product knowledge and etiquette weaved into face-to-face interactions at the point of sale.[2]

The term *personal selling* refers to the act of encouraging and facilitating a service transaction, face-to-face at the applicable point of sale. For some of us, the point of sale might be a boardroom, counter or reception desk. For others, it's a prospect's home or yard, or a restaurant floor. No matter where the selling is done, the seller's attitude and approach contributes enormously to a customer's POS experience. Our energy and aptitude (or lack thereof) has the power to amplify our business' success, or undermine it. Every opportunity to interact with a customer at the point of sale is a pivotal marketing opportunity. It's not only a chance to sell, upsell or cross-sell, but to build a bond and personalise the sales process, increasing the likelihood of repeat and referred sales into the future.

Thousands of resources are available to cultivate personal selling skills. *Secret Service Marketing* (the first book in the *Secret Service Business Series*) is an ideal starting point, with chapters dedicated to the improvement of attitude, professional presence and sales systems specifically. Beyond that, many books on sales, personal selling and the nuances of interpersonal communication can be found in libraries and bookstores, and a wealth of resources (both free and paid) are available online.

––––––––––––

The exciting thing about SSB survival activities – networking, prospecting, inbound telemarketing and personal selling – is that they can be overhauled instantly with no out-of-pocket cost. And the best part is that by implementing them, the likelihood of your business surviving to its next birthday (and beyond) can be boosted overnight.

CHAPTER 3.

NO-BRAINERS

In big business, paying for advertising comes with the territory. To generate the brand awareness required to stay top of mind on a global scale, you've got to pay for it... period.

Thankfully, promoting an SSB is different. SSBs need the awareness of a comparatively tiny target market (often in a designated geographic region), not the entire planet. There are better ways to achieve this than paid advertising – including several that can provide such a high return on investment that paying for advertising, without trying them first, would be crazy.

The trouble with paid advertising, and other marketing activities with a directly attributable, ongoing cost, is that their benefit is short-lived. As soon as we stop paying, our ads stop displaying – and when ads stop displaying, the leads stop rolling in. If paid advertising works, it becomes a relentless overhead cost with our business at the mercy of a media body. If it doesn't, we flush our hard-earned money down the drain. Either outcome is dangerous for a business with limited resources so, if we're able to, it's best to avoid paid advertising altogether.

This is possible by prioritising marketing tools and activities that involve an *upfront* and/or *occasional* investment of time or money, over those with a direct, ongoing cost. A Lead Machine website and sales kit are prime examples. Beyond their implementation, these tools continue to work time and time again with minimal effort or risk, providing an immeasurable return on investment over many years. Certain activities can do this too, providing a trickle feed or cumulative benefit with minimal ongoing effort and expense. From these, there is little to lose and much to be gained – to the extent we can consider them ***no-brainers***.

No-brainer activities are my favourite. In conjunction with a strong business model and equally strong marketing tools, they have the capacity to have an incredible impact, for a relatively miniscule investment of time or money. Activities that fall into this exciting category are summarised in the table below, then explained one by one.

Figure 4: No-Brainer Activities

Marketing Type	Marketing Activity (Opportunity)
Handshake Marketing	• Alliance Building
e3 Marketing	• Online Directories – Free Listings • Comparator Websites
Reputation Marketing	• Online Review Management • Public Relations Management
Search Engine Marketing	• Search Engine Optimisation – DIY
Local Area Marketing	• Point of Sale Promotion – Promotional Paraphernalia • Asset Advertising • Community Facility Advertising – Free or Low Cost • Resident Distribution Advertising – DIY • Local Markets
Guerrilla Marketing	• Celebrity Appeal Marketing

*** WARNING! DETAIL AHEAD ***
Chapters 3-5 contain detailed content that
may be overwhelming at first. If you get bogged
down in it, switch to skim reading and return
to each section as it becomes applicable.

Alliance Building

The most powerful and beneficial business relationships don't culminate in one
sale – they create an ongoing stream of
sales through the cultivation of mutually
beneficial alliances. A strong alliance can
change the course of business, providing
a steady feed of leads and sales.

There are three types of alliances most applicable to SSBs:

1. **A referral arrangement** – Where one business directs
   prospects or customers to another, for the provision
   of a service they can't, or don't want to, provide. The
   arrangement can be one-way (a specialist builder referring
   leads for general building services to a non-specialist
   builder) or two-way (a hairdresser and makeup artist
   mutually referring leads/customers to each other). If the
   referral arrangement is only one-way, a commission or
   spotter's fee may be paid as a reward for the referral, or the
   referred customer may receive a special offer or discount
   (benefitting the referring business by making it appear
   generous and well-connected).

2. **A joint venture (JV)** – This is when two or more
   businesses join forces, pooling their skills and resources
   to undertake a mutually beneficial marketing endeavour.

A joint venture could be created to submit a tender or grant application, for example, or to coordinate an event showcasing businesses in a particular region or industry (such as a regional wedding expo).

3. **An affiliate arrangement** – An agreement whereby businesses or individuals promote a product to their customers or contacts on behalf of the product's creator in return for a commission on resultant sales. Affiliate arrangements often involve information-based products such as books or online courses so they can be facilitated entirely online.

The emergence of social media has changed the game of alliance building, making prospective referrers, JV partners and affiliates more accessible than ever before. Through social media, lucrative business contacts and market influencers can be just a private message away. As with any form of networking, however, it's important to approach potential alliance partners as human beings, with the utmost respect and consideration, and to ensure your alliance proposition is strong and well thought-out before putting it on the table.

Alliances are some of the most important relationships a SSB owner can have but it's easy to get complacent and take them for granted. Like houseplants, most alliances require little attention to stay alive but with no attention at all, they will die. Keeping them alive and flourishing is as simple as:

- **Offering social rewards or opportunities** – Shouting your alliance partner an occasional coffee or lunch, or inviting them to an event you think may be of interest to them, such as a party, workshop or sporting event;
- **Gift giving** – Giving them an occasional gift, such as a bottle of wine on their birthday, to demonstrate

that you value them as a person and appreciate the alliance arrangement;

- **Reviewing the value of the alliance** – Taking time to reassess the monetary and non-monetary value of the alliance for each party to ensure it remains 'fair'.

As with personal relationships, a professional alliance should be mutually beneficial; providing relatively equal value to both parties. To achieve this, an ongoing investment of time and energy is required on both sides, in conjunction with trust and similar values – and the occasional gift doesn't go astray either.

Online Directories – Free Listings

Online directories provide a means for service seekers to find and connect with businesses of a particular type and location using the internet. Printed telephone directories once filled this role but online directories have left them in the dust, providing an immersive, user-driven search experience and more comprehensive business information, including hours of operation, customer reviews and photos.

Online directories vary in features and functionality. They can range from a simple, static list of business contact details – on the website of a business association, for example – through to dedicated directory/review sites such as Yellow Pages Online and Yelp. Dedicated directories usually provide the opportunity for a basic, free listing (the no-brainer option) and a more comprehensive, paid listing (explored in Chapter 5).

But the most powerful listing opportunities, by far, are those offered for free by the major search engines Google and Bing, with their platforms *Google Search, Google Maps* and *Bing Places*.

As far as marketing activities go, listing on Google Search and Maps provides an unbeatable return on investment. It's a means for businesses to get found and noticed online by service seekers in their local area, often resulting in a steady stream of leads and sales, with no out-of-pocket cost. To learn more about Google Search and Maps, and other free Google tools, refer to Chapter 20 of *The Secret Service Website Formula* – To Google, With Love: Free Tools to Get Search Traffic Sooner.

Bing Places is the local business directory provided by Microsoft's search engine, Bing. Although Bing has a substantially lower market share than Google, many computers and smartphones use Bing by default. For this reason, creating a free Bing Places listing can prove surprisingly worthwhile.

While Google Search, Google Maps and Bing Places provide the greatest e3 marketing opportunities for SSBs, there are countless free listing opportunities elsewhere. Most won't drive much traffic to your website but they will provide an opportunity to link back to it (important for SEO) and help your business dominate the first page of search engine results for your business name. Some of the most prominent directories are Yellow Pages Online, Yelp and TrueLocal – all of which are worth listing on. They are well optimised, which means they tend to rank well in search engines – usually appearing on the first page when a user performs a Google or Bing search for businesses of a particular type and location.

To take full advantage of free listing opportunities on online directories, complete all fields thoroughly and accurately and upload logo and photo files where indicated. If there's a description field, resist the temptation to copy and paste blocks of text from another website as you run the risk of breaching Google's duplicate content policy and adversely affecting your site's search engine performance. Instead, make the descriptions in directory listings as original as possible, tailoring them to the users of each platform.

For many SSBs, it's also worth considering classified advertising directories such as Gumtree, Craigslist or Facebook Marketplace. A free or low-cost ad on a classified advertising site can prove highly beneficial for certain service providers (particularly those offering trade, creative or personal services), as it's a means to tap into a stream of active, local service seekers. Just be aware that they're likely on the lookout for a bargain and, given that classified sites tend not to allow links to external websites, your Lead Machine website probably won't get the chance to subvert their sensitivity to price.

Even without posting ads, classified sites can be a source of leads by finding and responding to applicable 'wanted' ads posted by individuals seeking particular services. If you act quickly, you can jump on these leads and snap them up first. The process of searching for applicable ads can be automated by setting up search alerts on the various classified sites geared to notify you when ads matching specific criteria are posted.

Comparator Websites

Comparator websites orchestrate demand aggregation – a fancy way of saying they bring a pool of buyers and sellers in a particular market together

to facilitate transactions. They are sophisticated platforms, designed to compare the offerings, availability and prices of hundreds or thousands of businesses in a particular market, all in one place.

Comparator sites exist for all manner of services, from finance and fitness training to travel and trade services and everything in between. Some industries have one comparator site while others have many, battling it out for the lion's share of buyers and sellers in their market.

Some comparator sites, such as Tripadvisor, provide businesses with a basic, free profile or listing, whether they know about it or not, as do the major online directories.[3] This is done to present users with a full spectrum of service options. Investigating which online directories and comparator sites your business is listed on, then claiming ownership of those listings, is an absolute no-brainer. Once claimed, listings can be fleshed out with information and images, monitored for user activity (such as ratings and reviews) and managed accordingly. This helps make the most of the high-volume traffic generated by each site.

While some comparator sites are free, the majority exist by charging a fee or commission, depending whether they are **seller-driver** or **buyer-driven**.

On seller-driven comparator sites, sellers (service providers) initiate the buying process. Each seller presents a clear offer to the market, with predetermined pricing, then waits for buyers to respond. The comparator site makes money by charging a commission on any transactions initiated on the site.

Seller-driven comparator sites are incredibly powerful. In the accommodation sector, sites such as Trivago and Wotif have changed the game for small hotels and B&Bs, increasing their market reach and occupancy rates and putting them on an even playing field with larger, cashed-up competitors. Airbnb has added an extra twist to the market, making it possible for anyone with a spare room or residence to generate an income as a legitimate short-term accommodation provider. Seller-driven sites such as these have changed the face of the accommodation sector completely, as they have in many other industries.

Buyer-driven comparator sites revolve around the specific needs of individual buyers. Buyers initiate the process by posting a job or project on the site, then waiting for sellers to respond with quotes. Examples include Hipages, ServiceSeeking and Airtasker.

While they're all slightly different, most buyer-driven (job-based) comparator sites follow a process similar to this:

- A buyer (service seeker) posts a job/task on the site;
- Sellers (SSBs) are notified of the opportunity (lead) by SMS or email;
- Sellers interested in undertaking the work accept the lead and quote on it, paying a fee to the comparator site for the privilege;
- The buyer assesses the applicants, taking their quotes, profiles, job history and the feedback of previous buyers into consideration;
- The buyer awards the job to the seller that's most aligned with their needs and budget.

Despite comparator sites charging a fee or commission for facilitating anything beyond a basic listing, they are still a no-brainer. That's because most only charge you (the seller) when a service seeker chooses to transact with you, or when you choose to quote in response to a specific lead, so there's little to lose by giving it a go.

Before diving in though, prepare yourself for the fact that service seekers on comparator sites tend to be quite price-oriented. This can lead to disappointment for higher-end service providers who are repeatedly undercut by cheaper providers – particularly when paying for leads they're not winning. That said, many SSB owners with good communication and sales skills and/or a Lead Machine to take the emphasis off price, find comparator sites a godsend – providing the leads they need to stay busy and cash flow positive, all year round.

Online Review Management

In the game of modern marketing, *virtual* word of mouth is of greater concern than *verbal* word of mouth. Other than consistently providing an exceptional customer experience, we can't control what's verbally communicated about our business. What we *can* control, or at least strongly influence, is how our business is depicted and perceived virtually, through the activity of **online review management**.

The internet has amplified the age-old power of word of mouth. Experiences and opinions that would have once received limited, localised exposure are now globally visible via reviews on online directory, comparator and social media sites. These sites serve as platforms for web users to share their experiences and opinions of local businesses, both good and bad, en masse. While the implications of this may seem scary, a little bit of management can transform online reviews from a deadly foe into a precious marketing ally.

Anyone can post a review of a business online. They simply choose a review platform (Google, Bing, Facebook, YellowPages, Yelp, TrueLocal, Tripadvisor, etc), locate the business listing, select 'Write a review' (or equivalent), give a star rating from 1–5 and write a short statement to substantiate their rating.

Not only are these reviews publicly accessible, a business' average star ratings (good or bad) appear in Google Search results and Maps listings, as in the example below.

Figure 5: Google Search screenshot – 5-star listing
for Beggs Building & Pest Inspections (as at 26 Feb 2023)

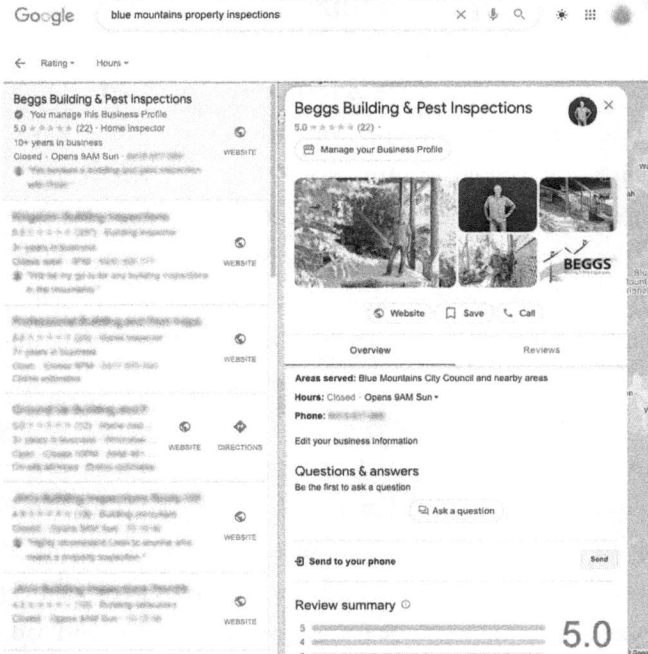

A business' average star rating (and quantity of reviews) can support or sabotage its marketing efforts. With a high rating, leads can flow in from search engines on autopilot – sometimes enough to sustain a business completely. With a low or non-existent rating, leads are lost to competitors with higher ratings.

For SSBs, a genuine 5-star rating on Google is more powerful than any fancy logo or catchy slogan. It's a visual representation of our business' standards, as perceived by those who have transacted with us in the real world. Our star rating is also an indication of the calibre of customers we're attracting. If we want 'easier' customers who are less sensitive to price, we need strong reviews and plenty of them. Like attracts like. Happy customers attract more happy customers.

4 Steps to Overhaul Your Online Reputation

Despite star ratings and reviews being a critical aspect of our SSB's identity, most of us don't give them enough, if any, consideration. A business' online reputation can undermine its marketing efforts for years, without its owner realising. A single negative review on an online directory (let alone a run of them) is all it takes for service seekers to dismiss the business and take their requirements elsewhere.

Luckily, taking control of a business' online reputation is not rocket science. Four basic tasks and a few minutes here and there are all it typically takes to transform your online reputation from a hindrance to one of your most valuable marketing assets.

TASK 1 – Monitor reviews

Managing reviews is an essential, ongoing process. A new review can pop up at any time, souring a previously impeccable reputation. Anyone can post a damaging online review – including a disgruntled ex-employee or jealous competitor posing as an unhappy customer to sabotage a 5-star or neutral (non-existent) rating. Actively monitoring your online presence is essential to nip negativity in the bud before it has a chance to impact business performance.

Google is the first port of call to monitor reviews. Start by searching for your business by name, as well as service type and location (e.g. 'plumbing Darwin') and notice what's displayed. Are any star ratings for your business displayed in search results? Do they help or hinder your online reputation? For each individual review, click the star rating to reveal the written detail and see what's been said.

Once a Google Business Profile (a business listing on Google Search or Maps) has been claimed, the business owner is automatically advised by email when a new review is posted. For other review platforms, it's worthwhile bookmarking each listing in an internet browser for quick access. This streamlines the task of checking them regularly – be it once a week or once a month, depending on the business and the likelihood of reviews being posted.

TASK 2 – Set Google Alerts

Not all reviews and comments are written on the major review sites – some are written in online forums such as Whirlpool, on blogs, or other sites. These can be found by Googling your business name, then scouring the search results for unsolicited comments or discussions.

Looking through search results is the easiest way to find pre-existing comments about your business but not the most practical way to monitor for new mentions into the future. Luckily, Google provides a handy, free tool that gives us the ability to monitor our business' internet presence with almost no ongoing effort. ***Google Alerts*** is a content change detection and notification service that keeps registered users informed of new instances of preset words or phrases (such as a business name) when they appear anywhere online. Once activated, email notifications are sent to you when Google finds web pages or publicly accessible online documents matching your specified search terms. Using Google Alerts is the simplest, most efficient way to know what's being said about a business or topic, within hours of it being shared online.

TASK 3 - Respond to reviews

Once a customer posts a review or comment, it's publicly visible for anyone online to see. But the story doesn't have to end there. Secret Service Marketers take things a step further, publicly replying to every review – good, bad or indifferent – as outlined below.

Positive reviews – Taking a moment to respond to a positive review (if the review site allows it), is good business practice. It makes the customer feel appreciated, while demonstrating your attentiveness and professionalism to the thousands of service seekers who will likely stumble across the review in years to come.

For maximum impact, avoid using a generic reply. Make each and every response unique and personalised – referring to the customer by name and referencing a detail or two from within the review to show it's been read thoroughly. For example, 'Thank you for your fantastic feedback, Louise. We hope to 'rock your tastebuds' again soon!'

Negative reviews – Many of us take an 'out of sight, out of mind' approach to bad reviews, preferring to bury our heads in the sand. Others can't help but bite back, making themselves appear immature and unprofessional in the process. Ignorance, defensiveness and dismissiveness are all extremely dangerous, as they validate negative reviews by default.

Instead of lashing out in anger, the best way to respond to a negative review is to take ownership and show accountability. Apologise for the fact that the customer feels disappointed. Acknowledge the problem as well as any lengths you went to to compensate the customer or alleviate their disappointment. Most importantly, state what you'll do, change or implement to reduce the chances of the situation happening again. Responding in this manner has the effect of antivenom on a toxic snake bite. It takes the sting out of the review, making it less likely to sabotage leads and sales into the future. A particularly well-crafted response can turn the tables completely – garnering the active support of potential customers reading the review who would otherwise become lost leads.

Fake reviews – Fake reviews can be alarming and disconcerting. They usually appear as a scathing 1- or 2-star review, posted under an obscure or false name so the critic's true identity is unknown. The written component of a fake review can be surprisingly well constructed and highly believable.

There are three steps to responding to a fake review:

1. **Reply** – Responding to any negative review, real or fake, is essential. With fake reviews, this can be done in a way that demonstrates that you take complaints seriously, while casting doubt over the validity of the review in the minds of those who come across it. *For example:* 'Hi *Reviewer Name*, we are so sorry to hear this and take your concerns very seriously. We have no record or recollection of any customer experience as recounted here however, nor do we have any record of a client with the name *Reviewer Name*, or variations thereof. If you were a customer of ours who was genuinely troubled by your experience, I ask that you reply with further information or contact *Owner/Manager name* on *phone number*, so we can discuss the issue, investigate where necessary and do what we can to alleviate your disappointment.'

2. **Flag/report** – Every review site has a method for reporting fake reviews. For some, it's a little icon in the shape of a flag, while others provide a 'Report' function. This can lead to the deletion of the review if the review site agrees it's illegitimate.

3. **Dilute** – If flagging/reporting the fake review doesn't get it deleted, the power of a 1- or 2-star rating can be diluted by encouraging happy customers to write reviews on the platform of concern to draw the average rating back up. The more 5-star reviews you accumulate, the less impact a bad one has; it will be perceived as an anomaly by potential customers and eventually become obsolete.

When starting out with online review management, it's a good idea for the SSB owner to personally respond to reviews and comments, in order to set the style and tone. Beyond the first few, the task of responding can be delegated to a suitable member of staff if desired.

TASK 4 - Use review invitations

While many customers may intend to leave raving reviews, few actually do. You can change this by introducing a simple paper-based flyer, given to customers at the end of each service transaction. In conjunction with a polite verbal request, a flyer detailing where and how to go about leaving a review (as per the example below) can significantly increase the proportion of customers who follow through with it. It's harder to forget about a physical flyer – handed over in earnest by an endearing business owner – than it is to forget about a purely verbal request or an email prompt sent days after the service has been provided. A physical invitation with clear instructions, given in person, is more likely to cultivate a sense of obligation, while making it as easy as possible to get the job done.

Figure 6: Draft of a customer review invitation

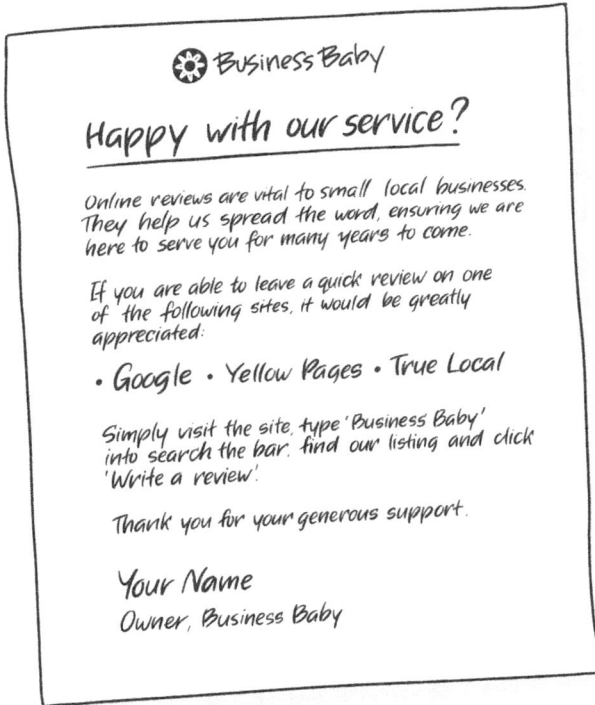

✳ Business Baby

Happy with our service?

Online reviews are vital to small local businesses. They help us spread the word, ensuring we are here to serve you for many years to come.

If you are able to leave a quick review on one of the following sites, it would be greatly appreciated:

- Google • Yellow Pages • True Local

Simply visit the site, type 'Business Baby' into search the bar, find our listing and click 'Write a review'.

Thank you for your generous support.

Your Name
Owner, Business Baby

Public Relations Management

Public relations (PR) management is often dismissed by small business owners as applicable only to big businesses. On the contrary, it's one of the most powerful marketing activities at our disposal.

PR management is concerned with the creation and maintenance of a favourable public image. For SSBs, there are three parts to it: 1) contributing to others, 2) capitalising on our contributions, and 3) counteracting bad press.

Contributing to Others

Great PR stems from contribution – giving our time, energy or expertise for the greater good of our community, industry, region or broader society.

SSBs can contribute in many ways:

- **Sharing a unique approach or solution** to a problem;
- **Winning an award** thereby drawing positive attention to a region or industry;
- **Coordinating/hosting a special event**;
- **Sponsoring** a community/industry event or initiative;
- **Donating services** for a good cause or the greater good (e.g. a builder repairing the home of a struggling family free of charge, or appearing as a trusted expert in a news segment about the dangers of old balconies);
- **Participating in a physical challenge** such as a triathlon or fun run to raise funds for a charity or cause;
- **Writing a column** for a local newspaper or trade magazine;
- And more.

Capitalising on Contributions

Contributing to others feels great on a personal level but for it to be of any real benefit to our business, it must be broadcast publicly. For some SSB owners, and in some cultures, this is an uncomfortable prospect. Modesty, introversion or a fear of 'tall poppy syndrome' can hold us back from sharing our contributions, let alone showcasing them. But, for the sake of our business, we need to take the plunge. This involves:

1. Getting media attention

Getting the contribution featured by mainstream media (TV, radio, newspapers or magazines) or online (blogs, newsfeeds, podcasts etc) can be very good for business – like striking marketing gold. While this can happen without prompting it, it's rare. Typically, media attention is garnered through tactical action, such as:

- **Sending media releases** – For a media body to consider featuring a story, they first need to be notified about it. This is done by writing and submitting a media release or concise 'news tip' to suitable media outlets. Generally, SSBs stand a greater chance of stories being picked up by local news outlets (community newspapers or radio stations, for example) but it's still worth notifying mainstream media channels. You never know, they just might run with it. Note that the chances of a story being deemed newsworthy are boosted by focusing your writing on the impact and benefits of your contribution – resisting the urge to angle for sales.

- **Inviting influencers** – If your contribution involves an event (a fundraiser, for example), its newsworthiness can be enhanced by inviting selected media personalities, representatives and influencers (celebrities, industry figureheads, bloggers, etc). Inviting strangers may feel awkward but if you don't invite them, you'll never know if they would have come and, in some way, altered the course of your business journey.

- **Embracing appearance opportunities** – Fully capitalising on contributions requires being open to media opportunities; TV or event appearances, interviews on radio shows or podcasts, photoshoots for newspaper or magazine articles, guest blogging or writing columns for applicable publications – anything that aligns with your values and raises your public profile. As nerve-racking as this may sound, remember: you can't build a successful business without ever leaving your comfort zone.

2. Identifying micro-marketing opportunities

Once a PR opportunity has been secured, a little extra planning can go a long way. Micro-opportunities are often available to:

- **Physically feature your brand** – Media appearances, events and other PR initiatives are a perfect opportunity for brand exposure, be it via branded uniforms, banners, vehicles, equipment, etc. Without basic branding (typically the business' name, logo and website address), there is no visual connection between your contribution and your business, squandering the opportunity for exposure.

- **Include a call-to-action** – A verbal call-to-action, such as 'Pete can be contacted through his website, *petespergolas. com.au*', can be appropriate in certain PR circumstances, however, it needs to be arranged with the interviewer or host first. An unsolicited 'plug' crammed into the close of an interview can do more harm than good, irritating the interviewer and undermining the generous nature of the contribution. A plug is infinitely more effective if the interviewer or host initiates it, rather than an obviously biassed interviewee.

- **Raise awareness before the big day** – Promoting an appearance or event in the weeks leading up to it through social media, email marketing and word of mouth helps squeeze more out of the opportunity. It can also increase attendance or audience numbers on the day (if applicable) and convey a sense of business momentum, amplifying the impact of the activity.

- **Make the most of your 'backstage pass'** – There's more to a media appearance than meets the audience's eye, including scores of micro-opportunities to take behind-the-scenes photos and footage. Visual proof of the recording studio, production staff and other media representatives – taken with permission – can serve as excellent fodder for blogging or social media activity. Note that photos and footage with you (the SSB owner) in them will generate more attention and a stronger response than those without.

3. Memorialising the media appearance

Without a permanent record of a media appearance, a monumental opportunity is lost – potentially costing tens of thousands of dollars in sales. There are two simple steps to memorialise it, giving it the capacity to have a positive impact on the market perception of your business for years or decades to come.

The first step is to obtain the media publication, be it a video or audio file, a scanned image of a printed article or, in the case of a blog or podcast, a screenshot with an accompanying link. The media body may provide this upon request but it's best to record or acquire it independently – just to be sure.

Once obtained, it's time for step two: making the publication a permanent, publicly accessible feature of your marketing communications by uploading it to your website. Footage, audio and image files can be embedded on a designated 'In the

Media' page, or in individual blog posts, depending how the site is structured. The link to this page can then be shared via social media, email and other means.

Embedding media articles and appearances on your website memorialises what would otherwise be a series of 'flash in the pan' occurrences. They give a sense of authority and legitimacy to your business identity and can have an astounding effect, boosting leads and sales well into the future.

As media articles and appearances accumulate on your website, it pays to add a visual snapshot of your media history to the homepage. This can take the form of a banner or feature strip containing the words 'Featured on...' or 'As seen on...' above the logos of the various media bodies you've been featured by. This one little addition to a SSB website can prove highly lucrative as it's a powerful form of social proof.

Counteracting Bad Press

Sometimes in business, undesirable things happen that can generate bad publicity – deterring people from engaging our services. A customer might get injured at our premises or find a band-aid in their burger. We might fail a health inspection or, for some reason, walk off a project without completing it. Left unaddressed, these events can plague a business for years and even drive it to closure.

Not responding to bad press validates the concern, so it's always best to face the issue head on – stepping up to the plate as a strong yet humble leader. Responding effectively to bad press starts by making contact with the media body that brought the issue to light and making yourself available for comment. If given the opportunity for an interview, show compassion, vulnerability and, most importantly, account-ability. Never blame or criticise. Apologise where apologies are due and outline what measures have been taken to ensure the same issue doesn't arise again. As with bad reviews, responding in a calm, considered way has the power to offset the negativity of bad press, helping the public forgive, forget and move on.

Search Engine Optimisation (SEO) – DIY

Search engine optimisation (SEO) refers to work performed on and around a website to help it rank higher in search engines, so it can be found by potential customers in search listings. A well opti-mised website is necessary to make the most of the opportunity to get search engine exposure without paying for ads. The better the SEO, the higher a website will rank in search engines for applicable search terms and the more free, organic traffic will flow to the site.

SEO can be outsourced to an external SEO manager or agency (presented in Chapter 5) or attempted internally, as a do-it-your-self (DIY) endeavour. The ability to get SEO traction as a DIYer largely depends on the nature of the service you provide and the geographic region you serve. In highly competitive markets – such as 'builders Sydney' – SEO success can be out of reach for DIYers, due to the sheer number of service providers vying for search engine traffic. In less competitive markets – such as 'gyprock repairs Nuriootpa' – getting traction can be easy, even for an SEO novice.

In markets with low to medium levels of competition, a few

simple SEO tasks – undertaken in-house with no out-of-pocket cost – can be all it takes to drive search engine rankings up exponentially. These tasks are (in my opinion) easiest to perform with a Wordpress website, as they can be executed and managed through the use of a single, purpose-built Wordpress plugin.[4] For other website platforms, a bit of online research will help determine if DIY SEO is an option, how effective it can be and how to get started.

As an aside, SEO is something we not only need to consider after our website goes live but long before – from the moment we start researching possible website platforms and designers. Certain platforms have built-in SEO advantages while others can hold a website back, preventing it from achieving the organic success that may be possible with a stronger foundation. For more information on choosing a suitable platform and/or designer, refer to Chapter 16 of *The Secret Service Website Formula.*

An SEO-friendly website platform and on-site SEO tasks are essential, but there's an 'off-site' side to SEO too. This often overlooked aspect is the utilisation of tools and systems, made available to website owners by search engines, to help our websites get found quicker and easier by potential customers. **Google Search Console** (previously Google WebMaster Tools) is one such tool. It allows us to push our website into the Google system so it gets indexed and listed in user search results quicker than it otherwise would.

The utilisation of Google Search Console and other free tools – shared in Chapter 20 of *The Secret Service Website Formula* (To Google, With Love: Free Tools to get Search Traffic Sooner) – can be more beneficial for SSBs than any other SEO task.

For some SSBs, using these tools in conjunction with a Lead Machine website is enough to rise through the Google rankings for relevant search terms and tap into a constant stream of hot leads. Others require more work. Either way, any time we invest exploring and implementing SEO is time well spent.

Point of Sale Promotion – Promotional Paraphernalia

Point of sale (POS) promotional para-phernalia refers to signs, displays, materials and other forms of visual communication geared to sell, upsell, cross-sell, incentivise or reward at the place where the sale is made or deal is done. Examples include counter displays, banners, posters, table talkers, specials boards, loyalty/rewards cards and more.

The thought of verbally enquiring about available offerings, specials, discounts or deals can be intimidating for customers, if they consider it at all. Having information and offers presented in physical form, provides them with a visual reference point and something to consider before engaging in conversation with a member of staff. It has the ability to simplify and streamline the purchasing process, contributing to a less stressful, more enjoyable customer experience.

That said, promotional paraphernalia should be geared to support the point of sale survival activity of personal selling (introduced in Chapter 2), not to outshine or replace it. Introducing a suite of well-considered POS materials can result in a worthwhile boost to our SSB's bottom line but it won't propel us to new heights of sales conversions and business growth like an overhaul of our personal selling approach can. As such, it's better to get the activity of personal selling on track before putting too much time or effort into promotional paraphernalia. It's okay for POS materials to be basic to begin with. They can, and should, evolve over time.

Asset Advertising

Asset advertising gives us a constant physical presence in our local community, through the adornment of business assets, such as buildings and vehicles, with promotional signage. This is one of the best marketing investments an SSB owner can make – providing immediate, ongoing advertising benefits, with no ongoing advertising costs. Asset advertising enables us to take advantage of passing foot and road traffic; generating exposure and awareness while going about our day-to-day business, not giving it a second thought.

Shopfront Signage

For SSBs with brick-and-mortar premises, asset advertising in the form of *shopfront signage* presents a major opportunity, so it's not a consideration to take lightly. Shopfront signage provides a visual reference point, making it easy for a business to be recognised and located. But beyond the logistics, it contributes to the general perception of a business – giving it the power to attract new customers and repeat patrons, or repel them.

A dated or faded front façade can silently undermine a business' marketing efforts by causing a sensory contradiction; making it look cheap when it's not. When a new customer realises a business is more expensive than they perceived from its shopfront, it's akin to false advertising, sparking 'till or bill shock' and a lingering sense of disappointment. This can overshadow the most positive of customer experiences; stifling hopes of positive word of mouth, repeat patronage and customer loyalty – all from outdated or poorly-considered signage.

Shopfronts don't need to be expensive to be effective. A bold paint colour paired with some simple, strategically placed signs and adhesive window decals, professionally produced by a signwriter, is all it takes to transform the perception of a business from cheap, old and out-of-touch to fairly priced, fresh and at the forefront of its field.

When planning shopfront signage, it's always good to feature the street number of the premises in a prominent position on the building, visible from the road. This is particularly important on long, busy streets, as it helps visitors travelling by vehicle spot the right building. It's also important to feature the business' phone number and website address in multiple locations, ensuring they are visible from all angles.

Vehicle Signage

While shopfront signage is applicable only for SSBs with a premises, the benefits of asset advertising are available to anyone who owns a vehicle. *Vehicle signage* presents an excellent advertising opportunity for SSBs of all shapes and sizes, including those run from home, freelance operations and hobby or side ventures. It can be particularly worthwhile for those providing mobile or in-home services whose vehicles spend a lot of time en route and parked in public places.

Most vehicles can be signwritten, from cars and utility vehicles through to heavy-duty work vehicles like bobcats and excavators. Determining if a vehicle is suitable for signwriting comes down to the amount of body and window space available on it and whether the vehicle complements or clashes with the market perception a business is trying to create. This generally rules out motorbikes and old cars but most other vehicles are open slather. Any vehicle in decent condition is a wasted advertising opportunity if left blank.

Vehicle signage can range from removable door signs to a full body wrap – a choice that's largely dependent on budget. A set of rectangular, magnetic door signs is the cheapest option. These are handy if you don't want to promote your business all day, everyday, as they can be removed and re-stuck as required. But they are small and restrictive – barely enough for basic business and contact details. At the other end of the vehicle signage spectrum is a full body wrap. These offer complete design flexibility, which means they give a vehicle the capacity to make a striking impression. Body wraps don't come cheap though, usually costing thousands of dollars. A middle ground on price and impact can be achieved by opting for a semi-permanent solution comprised of adhesive vinyl stickers. The strategic placement of individual letter and image stickers on various panels and windows can achieve the best of both worlds – excellent street appeal on a tight budget.

When planning vehicle signage, elements to consider including are:

- Your logo and/or business name;
- A slogan and/or dot point list of available services (for advice and examples, refer to Chapter 12 of *Secret Service Marketing* – The Truth About Branding);
- An incentive to take action, e.g. 'Free Half Hour Consultation' or 'Obligation-Free Measure & Quote';
- A clear, concise call-to-action with your phone number and website address, e.g. 'Phone us now on 0404 444 444 or visit ourwebsite.com.au';
- Accreditation or endorsement images, such as industry association membership or certification logos.

It's important to consider that your vehicle will be seen from various angles. All information should be visible from the rear, left and right. If operating in a busy city and regularly forced to wait in lines of heavy traffic, it can also be worth considering the front of the vehicle. Signwriting a back-to-front logo and website address on the front of a vehicle, so it can be seen by the driver of the car ahead when looking in their rear vision mirror, can squeeze that little bit more exposure out of your vehicle signage investment.

Community Facility Advertising – Free or Low Cost

Community facility advertising is a means to generate awareness and exposure for a business in its local community. The aim is to reach people in places where they convene to satisfy living or lifestyle needs – supermarkets, cafés, theatres, sporting grounds, etc.

A plethora of community facility advertising opportunities are available in most communities, including many that are free or very low-cost. Examples include:

- Pinning flyers to public notice boards at shopping centres;
- Leaving business cards or brochures at local eateries (with their owners' permission);
- Hanging advertorial signs on fences (with council/ landowner permission); and
- Being featured at charity events or in newsletters, in return for financial or 'in-kind' support of local organisations or initiatives.

Note that when you're approached to support a local event or fundraising initiative, it's better to contribute a voucher for the provision of goods or services to a certain value than to make a cash donation. Not only does this give your contribution greater impact – by shining a spotlight on the goods or services you provide – it's also much better for your business' bottom line and can result in the acquisition of delighted, new customers – primed for repeat patronage and positive word of mouth.

Although free and low-cost community facility advertising can be considered a no-brainer marketing activity, it's important to be realistic about it. The fact is, most community facility advertising initiatives don't reap big rewards. If you expect them to drive scores of leads, you'll be sorely disappointed. While they are worthwhile, it's best to undertake them with a spirit of generosity, community involvement and contribution, trusting that the exposure your business receives from them will amass over time, building an invaluable but intangible asset of goodwill.

Resident Distribution Advertising – DIY

Resident distribution advertising (RDA) involves the delivery of printed advertising materials to the letterboxes, doors, or driveways of homes or businesses in a designated region. It's easiest to facilitate through a community publication or distribution agency (covered later in Chapter 5) but due to the cost and commitment involved, there are a couple of DIY options to consider first.

Both of these DIY RDA opportunities involve preparing a bundle of flyers, selecting a geographic area, then walking from residence to residence distributing them. With the first, flyers (typically A5 or DL leaflets, or folded A4 brochures) are posted into letterboxes. This is commonly called a 'letterbox drop'. The second takes things a step further – knocking on the door of each home to deliver a flyer along with an in-person verbal spiel.

Letterbox Dropping

Letterbox drops are quite straightforward and have few downsides, other than their impact on the environment. Dropping flyers into letterboxes is a relatively quick, easy, non-intrusive activity, which can be repeated regularly if proven effective. The one downside – the environmental impact of printing flyers in bulk – can be reduced by choosing recycled paper and incorporating a recycle symbol into the flyer design.

Door-Knocking

Door-knocking has many more drawbacks. Firstly, it's subject to stringent consumer protection laws, such as those regulated by the ACCC in Australia.[5] These stipulate when door-to-door promotion is allowed and what protocols commercial door-knockers must comply with to avoid prosecution. But legal compliance isn't the half of it. Door-knocking – even on a couple of streets – takes much longer than letterbox dropping. It's also more emotionally draining.

Despite all of this, there is one instance in which the benefits of door-knocking easily outweigh its drawbacks: the launch of a new brick-and-mortar SSB. When a business with physical premises is launched – be it a takeaway food outlet, salon, motor garage, etc – it can take time for it to be embraced by the community. This can be expedited by humanising the business; capitalising on the personality and humanity of the new owner, so they and the business are perceived as one. Applying the Secret Service Website Formula is the best way to do this, but taking the time to knock on a few doors in the immediate vicinity can help get the ball rolling.

An introductory door-knocking campaign is not rocket-science. It just needs to be short, sweet, authentic and executed with confidence. A method that's easy to deliver, and likely to be well received, is as follows:

1. Explain who you are and where you're from (gesturing in the general direction of the business premises);
2. Advise that the business is new and if they have any concerns regarding street parking (or other applicable factors) to contact you directly;
3. Tell them you've got a flyer and a special VIP offer for them if they'd like it; and
4. If they accept, hand them a flyer and a business card with the special offer written on it – handwritten, signed and dated by you.

Even if only 5-10 residences are visited, this gets neighbourly relations off on the right foot and has the capacity to create a small base of customers and instantaneous advocates.

Top Tips for a Greater RDA Return

Although much cheaper than upper end alternatives, DIY resident distribution advertising is not free. The design and printing of flyers, plus the time it takes to distribute them, need to be taken into account. However, the return on your investment can be maximised by:

- **Producing a feel-the-love flyer** – Using *The Secret Service Website Formula* for reference, take a connective approach to flyer design by including a feel-the-love photograph and a short statement about your – or your primary technician's – professional accomplishments.
- **Luring them to a Lead Machine** – Give them a reason to visit your website with an enticing call-to-action, such as 'Visit us online NOW to download our menu / request a free quick quote / book a free 30 minute consultation'. This should be prominent on the page, along with the

website address in bold text – ensuring the 'www.' is included (to make it obvious that it's a website).

- **Including only basic contact details** – A website address and phone number are essential inclusions on an SSB flyer. Both can be repeated in multiple places but the phone number must always be the same, single number – not multiple options for landline, mobile, etc, as this can cause confusion. An email address should never be included, as this can stop service seekers from taking the preferable action of visiting your website. The business' physical address is only relevant if customers need to visit a brick-and-mortar premises to engage your services.

- **Accepting that 'no' means no** – 'No junk mail' and 'Do not knock' stickers should be respected at all times. Not only is it illegal to ignore them, it's blatantly disrespectful and aggravating to residents – inciting a negative perception of the offending business.

Note that more creative forms of resident distribution advertising are possible, such as placing flyers under the windscreen wipers of cars parked at certain locations or events. However, there's a risk of breaching local council regulations, incurring fines or penalties, and irritating your target market through a perceived disregard for the environment. So, be sure to weigh up the risks before getting creatively carried away.

Local Markets

A *local or community market* is a place where buyers convene to purchase locally produced goods and services from an array of sellers, set up at individual stalls. Local markets are typically held at the same time and location every week, fortnight or month, so they can become a renowned community event, attracting visitors from near and far.

Exhibiting at local markets is a no-brainer activity for many SSBs. Most obviously, it's ideal for artisans, growers, makers and bakers with physical goods to sell but it can be just as effective for service providers without tangible products. Markets can be great for those with the ability to deliver on-the-spot services, such as massage therapists or natural healers, as well as sporting clubs, builders and other service providers looking to increase awareness amongst local residents.

Local markets provide a myriad of networking and other marketing opportunities. For starters, regular participation demonstrates a commitment to the community and can foster valuable relationships with local residents, fellow stallholders and market organisers. Market stalls can also serve as testing grounds for new goods or services, providing the opportunity to qualitatively assess local demand before undertaking more expensive marketing activities.

But above all else, exhibiting at local markets provides the opportunity to have a physical presence in the community without having the overheads of a brick-and-mortar premises. To make the most of this and have the greatest impact, it pays to treat a market stall as a pop-up premises – adorning it with signage so it's easily recognisable and using point of sale materials and selling techniques to give it a unique and appealing presence.

Celebrity Appeal Marketing

Celebrity appeal marketing is a form of 'branding by association'. Being seen with or serving a celebrity leverages their celebrity status and social appeal, which can make us and our business seem 'cool' by association.

Big brands do this through high-paid endorsement deals – paying celebrities to use their products and represent them in advertisements, media appearances, etc, for a certain period of time. This may be outside the realms of financial possibility for most SSBs but it certainly doesn't render celebrity appeal marketing impossible.

Other than seeking to forge alliances with *celebrity influencers* (explained earlier), celebrity appeal can be generated by encouraging *celebrity appearances*. This takes a bit of audacity – proactively inviting celebrities to experience your services or attend applicable events. If they happen to accept and make an appearance, leverage it by requesting a few photos on the day. This process might feel daunting but there is nothing to lose by trying.

Some celebrity appeal marketing opportunities occur unexpectedly, without any prompting. A celebrity may walk into a café of their own volition, or request your services as a result of word of mouth. If this occurs, a quick decision is in order – to try and capitalise on the opportunity or not. This comes down to gut feel. If they look stern and avoid all eye contact, a request for a photo is likely to irritate them and – even if they are complicit – they'll never return. On the other hand, if they're friendly and engaging and it feels natural to ask for a photo, do it. If they agree, snap a quick selfie (making sure you're in the picture too), then give them the respect, anonymity and calibre of service extended to any other customer.

Celebrity photo opportunities don't have to stem from celebrities physically coming to us. Approaching them can be effective too. Attending external events such as launches, book signings or fashion shows, even those with no relevance to our business, can spark opportunities to meet celebrities and snap a selfie as visual proof of the interaction.

A visual history of authentic celebrity interactions and endorsements is a powerful addition to an SSB brand. It conveys a sense of momentum and activity and depicts us as a well-connected mover and shaker. Executed well, the appeal of celebrities we interact with can rub off on us, making us a bit of a celebrity in our own right, therefore more appealing to potential customers.

———————

In conjunction with a strong business model, a Lead Machine website and the survival marketing activities outlined in Chapter 2, a few well-considered no-brainer activities can be all it takes to comfortably sustain an SSB. Many no-brainers are largely 'set-and-forget', requiring minimal ongoing expense or effort. This makes them highly accessible and achievable; an ideal way to get a few runs on the board for those who are used to feeling daunted by the marketing function.

CHAPTER 4.

CHEAP BUT CHALLENGING ACTIVITIES

Aside from survival activities and no-brainers, a third set of low-cost marketing activities are worth the consideration of SSB owners – particularly those of us who fancy ourselves as budding entrepreneurs. Among these activities are some incredibly powerful marketing opportunities but they aren't everyone's cup of tea. That's because they require substantially more input and effort. They're cheap but they're challenging. As such, they are best suited to SSB owners with a high level of marketing ambition and energy, who can embrace the challenge of an activity and commit to it – recognising that it will require consistent effort over a sustained period of time to see a return on investment.

Figure 7: Cheap But Challenging Activities

Marketing Type	Marketing Activity (Opportunity)
Information Marketing	• Group Training • Content Marketing • Information Products
Social Media Marketing	• Social Media Activity
Direct Marketing	• Telemarketing – Outbound • Email Marketing • Mobile Marketing • Snail Mail Marketing
Guerrilla Marketing	• Viral Marketing • Street Marketing – Free or Low Cost

Before We Begin: What Information Marketing Really Means

As shown in the table above, ***information marketing*** is not an individual activity but one of the 10 types (spokes) of activity on the Marketing Wheel. As one of the newest types of activity available to SSBs, it's also one of the most misunderstood. Given that all three SSB-applicable information marketing activities fall together under the banner of cheap but challenging, there's no better time to clear up this confusion. So, before shining the light on each individual activity, let's look at it as a broader concept.

The underlying premise of information marketing lies in the following quote:

> 'If you want joy, give joy. If love is what you seek, offer love. If you want material affluence, help others become prosperous.' ~ Deepak Chopra

That might sound a bit too spiritual for a book about marketing but building an SSB is a commitment to a life of service – and a life of service is amplified by spiritual awareness.

Our SSB is merely an extension of us, which makes it subject to the same spiritual or universal principles. The energy we put out into the world – through a business or not – we get back in return (physically, emotionally, monetarily, etc). The more we put out, the more we get back. Information marketing is a means to contribute more, thereby amplifying our capacity to receive... financially and otherwise.

With information marketing, the energy put out is a blend of information and insight with the capacity to educate and empower others. This information can take many different forms (as we'll cover shortly). It can be disseminated online or offline, be free of charge or require monetary payment and be openly accessible or incentivised (offered as a reward for taking a certain action, such as providing an email address). Essentially, information can be offered with strings attached (only accessible once a payment of money or personal details are received) or without (accessible to anybody, free of charge or obligation).

For SSBs, the delivery of information *offline* – in a face-to-face workshop format for example – can have strings attached or not, at our discretion. The delivery of information *online* is different. We either need to offer it without strings, or reconsider our business model. When we start asking for payment or personal details in exchange for online information, it can muddy the waters of our business model – straddling the line between SSB and *information marketing business (IMB)*. This can be navigated successfully but requires careful planning in conjunction with the research and implementation of IMB-specific strategies.

Some of these will be touched upon in this chapter but not in great detail, so as not to confuse the owners of more traditional, local SSBs for whom the *Secret Service Business Series* is intended.

Whether information is delivered online or offline, the purpose of information marketing for SSB owners is to gently prime service seekers to engage our services by impressing them with our generosity, authenticity and expertise. It gives us the opportunity to familiarise them with our approach and methodologies, outline what they need to do to achieve a successful outcome and spell out what to look for when choosing a service provider (subtly implying they need look no further).

While the information we give away through information marketing may empower DIYers to undertake tasks or achieve certain outcomes for themselves, that is nothing to be afraid of. Those with the determination and desire to do it themselves are not your target market, nor will they ever be. So, let them go for it. Rest assured that equipping DIYers with the information they seek to undertake a project or achieve a goal independently is a happy, healthy byproduct of your information marketing efforts, not a hindrance to business success.

Having cleared that up, let's delve into the three information marketing activities of most relevance to SSBs: group training, content marketing and information products.

Group Training

Group training involves bringing a group of service seekers with a vested interest in a relevant topic together to educate, empower and inspire them to achieve

a certain outcome. Group training events can be presented as workshops, seminars, information sessions or even in-home 'parties' (depending on the business model and target market).

The facilitation and promotion of group training events can be one of the most effective marketing activities for SSB owners to employ. It has the capacity to position us as generous, trusted authorities or experts in our respective fields – transforming us into human magnets for leads and sales.

Not only can group training be highly effective, it's also highly efficient. Its 'one-to-many' structure leverages our time and resources by bringing us face-to-face with many potential customers at once. It gives us the opportunity to engage, educate and impress multiple individuals in the same amount of time, or less, than it can take with one.

Group training is often overlooked as an information marketing opportunity because – unlike others – it's delivered offline, in person. However, thanks to online platforms such as Eventbrite and WeTeachMe, which facilitate the logistics of event management and registration, it's seeing a definite resurgence and will continue to do so, post-pandemic.

As an SSB owner, one of the best things about running group training events is being forced to articulate what you do and how/why you do it, in a way that's easy for an audience to understand. This can result in the development of valuable models and formulas that become the basis for information products (books, courses, etc) later down the track. It also has the ability to advance your business by exposing a niche market or refining your marketing message.

On a personal note, it was in preparing the slide decks (PowerPoint presentations) for group training workshops that the Busy/Slow Cycle, Marketing Wheel, Secret Service Website Formula and other Secret Service concepts were conceived. Not only did these models and theories change the course of my struggling business and the businesses of my clients, they were the catalyst for fulfilling a lifelong dream to write a book (or set of books, as it turned out). It's quite amazing where the preparation of a workshop and some out-of-the-box thinking can lead.

As a marketing activity, group training sessions are usually free to attend. Running free events can be incredibly rewarding but it's not without its challenges – the greatest of which is the art of getting 'bums on seats'. The majority of attendees who register to attend free events (often in the realm of 50–70%) simply don't turn up. Without anticipating and preparing for this by strategically 'overbooking' the event, it can be a disappointing and costly experience.

Of course, there's always the option to charge a token amount for group training events. Paying for a ticket makes registrants more likely to show up as they're more invested, however they have to be extremely interested to sign up in the first place.

If interested in group training as a marketing activity, but concerned about getting bums on seats, consider forging a collaboration with an applicable organisation that has an established member/client base. Local business, trade and industry associations are often on the look-out for trainers to present on topics of interest to their members. They generally charge attendees a small fee to attend a session, expect trainers to provide their speaking/training services for free and prohibit the blatant promotion of services but, rest assured, it's still very much worthwhile.

For business-to-business (B2B) service providers, the best case scenario is a collaboration with an association that facilitates **professional development training**. This means it provides training opportunities for members that help them satisfy the obligations of a professional accreditation or licence. Each training event they attend earns them a certain number of professional development points or hours, helping them to reach a predetermined annual minimum. If they don't attend enough training sessions, they can't accrue enough points, and if they don't accrue enough points, they lose their licence. There is no better incentive to attend a training event than that.

It can be harder to fill a group training event without a strategic collaboration but certainly not impossible. A compelling topic, clever copywriting and a tangible incentive or two – such as a free goodie bag and complimentary food and drink – can go a long way to getting bums on seats.

Content Marketing

Content marketing is the act of creating and publishing online content, specific to our field of expertise, for free. The aim is to attract and retain the attention of internet users, build a strong online profile and ultimately (but indirectly) drive sales.

The Content Marketing Institute explains it best:

> 'Content marketing is the art of communicating with your customers and prospects without selling. It is non-interruption marketing. Instead of pitching your products or services, you are delivering information that makes

your buyer more intelligent. The essence of this content strategy is the belief that if we, as businesses, deliver consistent, ongoing valuable information to buyers, they ultimately reward us with their business and loyalty."[6]

Types of Content

Content can be split into five categories:

- **Authored** – Content consumed (primarily) through reading, such as the words on websites, blog posts, articles, ebooks, bonus chapters, how-to guides, whitepapers, reports and checklists.
- **Auditory** – Content consumed by hearing, such as podcasts, recordings, audiobooks, audio lessons and courses, ringtones and music tracks.
- **Visual** – Content consumed (primarily) through sight, such as photographs and other images, slides/presentations and infographics.
- **Video/multimedia** – Content comprising moving images, usually with accompanying audio. It includes recorded video, live video streams, animations, educational webinars and more.
- **Interactive content** – Content that requires input or action from the user to derive value from it. Examples include tests, quizzes, tools and calculators, polls and surveys, software, games, fonts, patterns, templates and other files.

All five types of content can be used to support a business' online marketing efforts. For SSBs, authored, visual and video content tend to be the most beneficial – particularly when featured on the business' own website. As detailed in *The Secret Service Website Formula*, the text, images and videos on an SSB's website – the hub of its marketing activity – can make or break its marketing efforts. They are a crucial consideration and a higher priority than any of the 10 spokes of the Marketing Wheel.

However, this particular book is about the spokes of the Wheel, not the hub. As such, we'll discuss content as it pertains to the activity of content marketing, not the creation and population of a website. The big difference between the two is that content produced for a website is more promotional, while content produced for content marketing purposes is more educational; created with no financial agenda, for the greater good.

Content marketing takes place beyond the core pages of a business' website. It's geared to build brand awareness on external internet platforms (search engines, social media, etc) and subtly lure internet users (including potential service seekers) back to the main pages of a website. Note that content provided as part of a sales pitch (such as an online sales page or webinar), or offered for sale as paid content (an information product), falls outside the scope of content marketing because it's not free or 'communicated without selling'.

With the above in mind, the two types of content marketing most applicable to SSBs are *authored* and *video* content marketing.

Authored Content Marketing – aka 'Blogging'

Authored content marketing involves the production of written content for online publication – usually posts for a ***blog***. A blog (short for weblog) is a collection of text-rich articles pertaining to a particular topic or field of interest, typically accessible via a link in a website's navigation bar. Blog posts are predominantly text-based with one or more images, videos or other types of content to help them engage, educate or entertain.

Google and other search engines love blogs. They tend to rank highly in search listings due to the rich, user-centred nature of the content they contain, and can help the more promotional pages of an SSB site gain traction too.

Logistically, blogging is easy. It's particularly easy with a Wordpress website, as blog posts can be created from the same dashboard used to maintain the site's core pages.

The logistical ease and SEO benefits of blogging make it an attainable and potentially invaluable strategy but, like other cheap but challenging activities, it's not everyone's cup of tea. Effective blogging is a labour of love. It takes time and effort to plan, write, refine and publish one blog post – let alone one every week or month, on an ongoing basis. Drive and dedication are essential, as well as an ability to push through any feelings of disheartenment that stem from seeing no direct benefit from your work, because letting a blog lapse can look worse than no blog at all. A few old posts on an SSB website can imply that you're unmotivated, out of business or – at the other end of the spectrum – too busy to give service seekers the attention they deserve.

Luckily, blogging for your own website is not the only option. A less demanding but equally beneficial alternative can be to serve as a *guest blogger*. This involves writing posts for blogs run by third party individuals or organisations, rather than writing them for your own site. Although the SEO benefits of guest blogging aren't as strong as independent blogging, it can help generate credibility and a flow of traffic to your website without the ongoing investment of time and energy required to run a decent, independent blog.

Before reaching out to a third party blog owner to introduce yourself however, do your due diligence. It's important to consider: 1) the blog's reputation, 2) its relevance to your target market, 3) if it aligns with your values, 4) the amount of traffic it generates, and 5) whether it gives guest bloggers the opportunity to link back to their own site. Without investigating these five points, you could end up giving away your highest quality written content without a trace of traffic in return.

Video Content Marketing

Like authored content marketing, *video content marketing* involves the creation and sharing of free content in an effort to attract and retain an online audience and ultimately (but indirectly) drive sales. However, instead of posts written for a blog, videos are produced for publication via social media. Video content marketing is a strategy often pursued by SSB owners seeking to transition (knowingly or not) to an internet marketing business (IMB) model for personal or business services such as coaching, self-development or fitness training.

The most common forms of video content marketing for SSBs are self-produced *on-the-run* videos and semi-staged *educational* videos. The most effective of these are geared to remove the veil of a business' operations – providing useful, valuable content about applicable topics, with no expectation of monetary return. This often involves sharing expert insights or demonstrating a tool or technique, thereby empowering viewers to attain a certain outcome for themselves.

On-the-Run Videos

An *on-the-run video* is the multimedia version of a business owner selfie. Typically recorded on a mobile phone, with no real thought to lighting, staging, editing etc, an on-the-run video is produced to convey a short, verbal message. On-the-run videos are most commonly dispersed to an existing audience via Facebook, Instagram or TikTok, where they tend to be here one day and gone the next.

Educational Videos

The aim of an *educational video* is to provide useful or practical information to viewers, empowering them with knowledge. An educational video is usually a step up from an on-the-run video in terms of both production (lighting, staging, editing, etc) and content (planning, preparation, depth of purpose and resultant usefulness). It might include a series of comprehensive, well-structured insights or instructions about a particular topic, an interview with an industry expert, a physical demonstration of a task or activity, a product road-test or review, or a combination thereof. Educational videos are best published via a YouTube channel where they have the opportunity to: 1) generate organic views and channel subscriptions, 2) be shared on other online platforms such as websites and social media, and 3) lead viewers back to a website via a link.

Although a YouTube channel of educational videos requires more planning and prioritisation than the occasional on-the-run video on Facebook, it's a more powerful content marketing strategy. Not only does it result in higher quality, more useful videos, it enables them to remain relevant, accessible and useful indefinitely – providing an ongoing marketing benefit.

Because educational videos are generous in nature, they are a great way to establish yourself as an authority in a particular field or topic, build trust and generate business awareness. As they are highly visual and engaging, they also tend to provide a more direct benefit in terms of leads and sales than authored content marketing strategies like blogging. For service providers with the capacity to deliver services remotely – coaches, counsellors and tarot readers, to name a few – video content marketing has changed the game, with those who are generous with their time and expertise (via free online videos) generating more leads and building more sustainable businesses than those who aren't.

As with blogging however, video content marketing is an exercise in commitment, consistency and delayed gratification. Although it can be highly effective, it requires an active commitment to the production and distribution of new videos. Even when no-one seems to be 'picking up what you're putting down', new video content needs to be prioritised, planned and produced regularly with an attitude of patience and persistence. The tenacity required to succeed with video content marketing is exemplified by globally renowned coach and self-described multi-passionate entrepreneur, Marie Forleo, who produced and distributed educational videos for years before gaining enormous momentum with her YouTube channel, MarieTV.

While the global reach of video content marketing was the right path for Marie, it's not for everyone... nor does it need to be. For those of us whose SSB operations are confined to a small local region due to the nature or logistics of our service, who have no intention of morphing from an SSB to an Internet

Marketing Business or who can't think of anything worse than live streaming to TikTok, there are other ways to reap an ongoing reward from video, without an intense, ongoing commitment – namely, the use of **website enhancer videos**.

Website enhancer videos are not a form of video content marketing – nor a marketing activity at all. Rather, they are a means to enhance a website's performance as a marketing tool, boosting its ability to function as a Lead Machine. There are three types of website enhancer video applicable to SSBs – each one an optional extra in terms of website content. As explained in Chapter 6 of *The Secret Service Website Formula*, The Vigour and Virtue of Video, two of these are well worth considering. Done well, they have the capacity to boost your bottom line for many years without adding much, if anything, to your ongoing workload.

––––––––––––

The decision to pursue content marketing is not one to take lightly. Determining the type and frequency of content to create and share is a highly personal process, which requires self reflection. Not only do you need to consider the time and energy you have available to commit to content creation and be honest with yourself about your expectations and motivations, you might also need to challenge some underlying beliefs surrounding your suitability for creating content, such as a lack of confidence in your writing style or video presence. When it comes to content marketing, there's no right or wrong decision – only what's right for you.

Information Products

One of the most intriguing activities for fledgling entrepreneurs is the creation and sale of a bundle of paid or incentivised content, known as an *information product*. Predominantly sold and delivered online, information products commonly take the form of books, reports, video series', courses, memberships or webinars.

Creating an information product can take a substantial amount of time and energy but, once complete, exponentially amplifies our capacity to help others – turning our knowledge and expertise into a product. If the product has strong appeal and is well promoted, it can generate income and residual benefits for years, or even decades.

Like a chunk of meat on a pole entices a crocodile to jump out of the water, an information product acts as a lure to generate a desired response (either to purchase the product or subscribe to a list). Website users won't jump for just anything though; the content must convey a sense of quality and value. It must be a tender, juicy meal.

Books: The Ultimate Information Product for SSBs

There are few better ways to stand out from the crowd in a competitive service industry than writing and publishing a book. It's no mean feat but producing a high-quality book is a powerful marketing strategy. A published writer is perceived as an authority in their field, which, for an SSB owner, can be extremely good for business. There's no better claim to fame than having literally written the book on your field of expertise. It gives service seekers an immediate sense of security, reducing the perceived risk of buying from you and boosting the chances of them engaging your services.

A book can serve as a ***gateway product***. In buying it, service seekers make an important leap from *prospective* customers to *paying* customers. This gets them comfortable transacting with you, so they'll be more likely to engage in larger transactions down the track.

However, not just any book works as a gateway product. For best results, it should serve a clear and useful purpose to the reader – educating or empowering them with a system or methodology to achieve a definite, desirable result. The common temptation to feature the author's face on the front of the book should be avoided. This implies that the book is focused on the writer, rather than a source of information and inspiration for the reader. An autobiography or photographic coffee table book generally won't have the same effect as a highly informative 'trade book', as it will be perceived as an unnecessary optional extra.

The higher quality a book is, in both content and cover design, the more successful it will tend to be. While a myriad of courses and coaching programs have sprung up in recent years to help business owners write books in the shortest possible time, be aware that most nonfiction authors don't unearth or articulate the true gold of their knowledge and intuition until the second draft, with many requiring three or more drafts, followed by professional editing and design to produce a work of genuine value and appeal. Instead of looking for shortcuts, just start writing and don't stop until you feel genuinely proud of what you've written. Take comfort in the fact that writing a book is not supposed to be easy. As best-selling author Cheryl Strayed says:

> 'Writing is hard for every last one of us, straight white
> men included. Coal mining is harder. Do you think
> miners stand around all day talking about how hard
> it is to mine for coal? They don't. They just dig.'[7]

With a solid concept, patience and persistence, there's no reason you can't produce a work of nonfiction genius, capable of putting you on the entrepreneurial map.

Writing a quality book may be an unavoidably tough slog but – thanks to the internet – publishing and selling it is easier now than ever before. Not only has the internet made it possible for readers to find, purchase and read books about anything, from anywhere, it has made it far more feasible for authors to produce and publish their own works.

Making a book available in both electronic and printed formats is ideal. While ebooks are still popular with some readers, printed books are making a comeback – particularly in nonfiction genres. Not only that, publishing a book in a physical format gives its author more credibility – a vital consideration for books produced by SSB owners as an information marketing endeavour.

Printed books are perceived to be more difficult to produce and coordinate than ebooks but that's no longer the case. The internet has changed the face of book publishing and distribution. Now, there's not much more involved in producing and distributing a physical book than there is an ebook. This is due partly to the availability of online book design services and layout tools, such as Pressbooks, but mostly to the evolution of **print-on-demand** technologies.

Print-on-demand has streamlined the logistical processes of book distribution and delivery, making self-publishing a much more feasible pursuit. Now, when a book is ordered, anywhere in the world, one individual copy is printed and bound at the nearest printing house and shipped directly to the customer, bypassing the author. With a print-on-demand service such as IngramSpark (the self-publishing arm of LightningSource) or CreateSpace (affiliated with Amazon), it's possible to distribute books all over the world without actually ordering or storing any. This is exciting for SSB owners. It means we can make an otherwise small-scale information product available to a global market with no minimum order quantities, no geographic borders and no need to be picked up by a traditional publisher.

That's not to say that traditional publishing is no longer worth considering. For those seeking to share a message or formula for the greater good (as opposed to driving sales to a business), traditional publishing can be a viable option – providing extra support, exposure and a greater sense of authority. However, for those seeking to publish a book as an information marketing activity (to drive more business), self-publishing through a print-on-demand service such as IngramSpark or a small, third party agency is the ideal means to make it happen. Just be sure to avoid international vanity publishing scams (Google it – get informed before getting ripped off).

Other Information Products

Besides books, an array of information product options are available to SSBs. As mentioned at the start of the chapter, running paid training workshops can be an excellent way to generate exposure while creating an additional income stream. However, there must be enough demand for our teachings that people are prepared to pay to attend; more feasible for a cake decorator or florist than a lawyer or funeral director.

For the more entrepreneurial amongst us – intrigued by the idea of moving to a less traditional business model and not afraid to get some digital dirt on our hands – a more interactive online information product could be on the cards. This can take the form of:

- **An online course** – Online courses are structured training programs, delivered via a training hub or portal, designed to help students/clients develop a specific skill or achieve a certain result. A course is usually broken down into a series of topics or modules to make it easy to comprehend and work through. A module typically contains a combination of video or audio lessons, presentations (slide decks) and supporting documents.
- **A membership site/subscription or coaching program** – Like courses, membership sites/subscriptions and coaching programs also help students/clients develop a skill or achieve a result but in a less structured format. In lieu of regimented lessons, they typically offer the ongoing guidance of a coach or mentor and/or the support of an online community of like-minded members through videos, members-only forums or hangouts, conference calls, question and answer (Q&A) sessions, checklists, downloads and more.
- **A webinar** – Webinars are seminars broadcast over the internet . A webinar can be an information product in its own right, delivered for educational purposes, or it can have a promotional twist – discussed shortly.

Besides their format and modes of delivery, the main difference between books, online courses, membership sites/subscriptions and coaching programs is the amount of effort required to manage and facilitate them. With books and basic online courses, the bulk of effort is required upfront. Once created and published, they are essentially set-and-forget, requiring little modification and management from one year to the next. Membership sites/subscriptions and coaching programs exist at the other end of the set-and-forget spectrum. With them, creating the base product is just the beginning. They are a business unto themselves. Members and coaching clients expect fresh new content to be delivered regularly, as well as a certain level of responsiveness and support to justify their subscription. For an SSB owner, this requires a shift in focus and mindset – from the provision of physical services to the provision of online, information-based services... an entirely different kettle of fish.

This shift can be navigated and prove extremely lucrative but it requires a change in business model. Selling information-based products via the internet requires different skills, systems and strategies to those required to sell physical services in the real world. It requires an IMB model, not an SSB model.

Building an IMB appeals to a lot of aspiring entrepreneurs, and rightly so. IMBs have minimal setup costs, staffing requirements and customer interaction, are extremely scalable and not limited to any one geographic region. Competition can be fierce but usually amongst those who lack experience, integrity and authenticity. Individuals with extensive experience as SSB owners are some of the best equipped to transition to, and succeed with, an IMB.

IMBs thrive on systemisation and automation. Just as the internet has changed the game of book publishing, it has opened up a world of possibility for the delivery of information products. An array of digital platforms, such as Teachable, Zippy Courses, Patreon and Memberful have been developed to facilitate the sale of online courses and memberships. If considering the development of an online information product, it's a good idea to start by researching these and similar platforms, paying attention to what other SSB owners have achieved with them. There are many eye-opening and inspiring stories attesting to what's possible with a bit of tenacity and willingness to think outside the SSB box.

Using webinars to promote information products

One of the most valuable platforms in an information marketer's stack of systems is software designed to facilitate *webinars*. With the right webinar technology, we have the power to transcend time and space, extending the potential audience of a live presentation across the globe and into the future. Cloud-based platforms such as WebinarJam, WebinarNinja, EasyWebinar and GoToWebinar can be geared not only to handle complex before, during and post-webinar logistics but to facilitate automatic re-streaming of the event, on autopilot – allowing us to capitalise on a single webinar for months or even years.

For IMBs (or SSB owners considering a transition to an IMB model), webinars can form an integral component of an online marketing funnel. With a high-quality information product, the right software, a well-promoted, informative presentation and a strong call-to-action, webinars aren't just a good idea for IMBs – they are a no-brainer marketing activity.

Using freebie products as a lure to build a list

For SSBs *without* an information product to sell, incentivising online content (offering a free ebook in exchange for a website visitor's email address, for example) is pointless, and can even be detrimental. Building a list of subscribers by enticing them with a free information product is an undeniably powerful strategy for IMBs with information products to sell, but for SSBs delivering physical services in a localised area, it's futile. It tends to build a list of individuals outside our business' target market (such as DIYers and competitors fishing for information), if it builds one at all. If we want to build a high-quality list of individuals with a genuine interest in and ability to engage our services, it's best to steer clear of incentivised online content and invest our time and money in more beneficial marketing pursuits.

––––––––––––

Information marketing can seem counterintuitive to those with a more traditional business mindset but the days of holding our cards close to our chests are gone. Succeeding in the modern world of marketing requires a spirit of trust and generosity; trust that being transparent will *make* our business, not *break* it, and that in giving freely of our insights and expertise, we will eventually receive.

At a bare minimum, information marketing requires an interest or enjoyment of writing, creating or teaching, as well as time and patience. Many of us don't have that; we want to stick to what we know, love and do well in the physical world, and that's perfectly okay. However, for those who are open to exploring the world of information marketing, investing in self-education and applying some online elbow grease, a world of opportunity awaits.

Social Media Activity

As briefly introduced in Chapter 1, the spoke of social media marketing comprises two options: paid social media *advertising* and free social media *activity*. While both are worthy of consideration for SSB owners, the latter (social media activity) should be considered first, as it provides the opportunity to generate business with no out-of-pocket cost.

Social media activity involves the development and engagement of an audience of followers via a business page or profile on one or more social media sites. These can include Facebook, Instagram, LinkedIn, Pinterest, TikTok, X and more. Engaging in social media activity is free on every social media site, making it one of the cheapest and most alluring marketing activities. However, it can also be one of the most challenging.

While most of us could name several SSBs that would struggle to survive without social media, we're just as likely to name others (our own included, perhaps) that have found it a complete waste of time. This disparity is not a figment of our imagination, nor is it necessarily a reflection of the respective time and effort put into building each business' social presence. It's just the reality of modern marketing. Being active on social media proves priceless for some businesses yet worthless for others.

Finding success with social media is not luck of the draw, however. Some SSBs – and their owners – are simply better suited to social media activity than others. To avoid sinking time and energy into a cheap but challenging activity that's not suited to us (and therefore not capable of reaping a decent return), we need to assess this suitability upfront. The Social Suitability

Quiz provided in Chapter 15 of *Secret Service Marketing* (The Social Media Timetrap) is a tool developed to do just that.

It's important to understand that a high social suitability score and a commitment to post updates regularly is not enough to take social media by storm. No matter how often you post, you're not guaranteed to generate exposure for your business beyond your base of followers, or even within it – that's what **social media advertising** (the paid social media marketing option) is for. What *will* boost your exposure and unleash your social media potential is prioritising the *quality* of updates over the *quantity* of updates. It's not how often you post but the capacity of those posts to inspire heartfelt social connections that counts.

Social media should never be ignored – even by those with low social suitability scores, or who aren't geared for full-steam social media activity. As explained in *Secret Service Marketing*, a **listing presence** or **supporting presence** is often a better choice than a full-scale **driving presence** and is always better than no presence at all. Whatever you decide upon, one thing's for sure – it'll be infinitely more beneficial than burying your head in the social media sand.

Telemarketing – Outbound

Outbound telemarketing uses the phone to initiate verbal contact with potential customers and business contacts, for the purpose of generating or sustaining business.

The most extreme form of outbound telemarketing is **cold calling**. Cold calling involves phoning people deemed to be in your target market, out of the blue – with no prior relationship or advance warning – to push a predetermined, sales-oriented agenda. Once upon a time, cold calling was considered a test of business tenacity. The more cold calls we made, the more committed and determined we were, and the more likely we were to be successful (financially, at least). Luckily for those of us who feel overcome with dread at the thought of cold calling, times have changed.

Making cold calls is no longer the fruitful marketing activity it once was. Few people are receptive to being approached and sold to by strangers over the phone – and our potential customers are no different. Cold calls typically induce feelings of stress and anxiety for the caller and intrusion, irritation and scepticism for receivers – not the best basis for an enduring business relationship. As such, cold calling tends to be a poor investment of an SSB owner's limited time and energy.

That's not to say we should write outbound telemarketing off, however. In other forms – ones that make better use of our time and induce less anxiety – it can be incredibly beneficial.

The two outbound telemarketing activities of most benefit to SSBs tie back to the survival activity of manual sales prospecting. They are:

1. **Warm calling (phoning prospective customers or connections, with justification)**

   Warm calls are similar to cold calls but with a crucial difference... the chill is taken off the call by highlighting a personal, logical connection between the caller and receiver. For example: 'Hi Kate, my name is David Johnson. I was speaking with Jacinta Spring yesterday and she suggested we connect with each other, so I thought I'd give you a call.' The best way to warm a call is to reference a trusted third party individual or organisation. As long as the referral is genuine (not falsified or inflated), the mood of the call will instantly lift. It justifies the interruption, cuts through scepticism and paves the way for a relationship-based proposition – such as meeting for a coffee. This strategy is particularly effective for establishing alliances.

2. **Hot calling (phoning past and current customers)**

   Phoning those who've already engaged your services is one of the cheapest and most beneficial direct marketing activities. Simple things like keeping a client in the loop about the status of their project, following up with them weeks or months after the service has been delivered, and checking in with those who haven't been in contact for a while, can make a world of difference to customer retention and referral rates. It's far easier and more cost effective to generate sales from those who've previously transacted with us than those who haven't; the phone just happens to be the most direct, socially acceptable and effective means to make it happen.

If determined to try cold calling, note that outbound telemarketing is subject to stringent consumer protection regulations, along with other invasive activities such as door-knocking and approaching people in public places. To avoid the potential legal ramifications of cold calling, it's wise to investigate these regulations before dialling.

The most important thing to recognise before your next phone call is that telemarketing is no longer about pushing goods or services onto unsuspecting sales prospects. It encompasses any use of the phone to initiate, build, support or maintain business relationships. Every call we make presents an opportunity to build or bolster a relationship and improve the perception of our business. The more we embrace the phone as a marketing tool, the stronger and more sustainable our business will become.

Email Marketing

Where telemarketing uses the telephone to generate and sustain business, *email marketing* uses email or *EDMs*. Short for *electronic digital mail*, an EDM is an email prepared and sent to a group of contacts on a mailing list in the interest of business awareness, salience or promotion.

Internet marketers say 'the money is in the list'... and the same holds true for businesses in the real world. Once someone's details are in our mailing list, we have the ability to contact them via email to build upon the relationship – providing access to useful content, rewarding them with special offers and reminding them of our business' existence, with almost no out-of-pocket expense. Powerful stuff.

That said, we don't want every Tom, Dick and Harry on our list. For SSB owners – particularly those restricted to a certain geographic area – it's better to have a small, high-quality and legal list of customers and contacts, than an enormous, old or unlawful list of strangers who are unlikely to engage your services.

Building a high-quality mailing list involves lawfully collecting and storing the details of:

- Customers;
- Contacts;
- Sales prospects;
- Event registrants;
- Others who show an interest in engaging your services (beyond a polite, socially acceptable level of interest).

A mailing list can be retained in various ways, from a simple spreadsheet or database to a more sophisticated, paid system. A cloud-based email marketing or ***autoresponder*** service such as Mailchimp can be ideal for SSBs – costing little, if anything, to run. Scores of more comprehensive systems are also available – ConvertKit, Active Campaign and Constant Contact to name a few. Many of these systems have customer relationship management (CRM) and advanced marketing options geared more towards IMBs than SSBs. Because of this, it's important to weigh up the price and features of various systems carefully, ensuring you don't get stuck paying a higher fee than necessary for fancy features you'll never use.

A well-maintained mailing list is a valuable asset. It gives us the ability to communicate with potential customers through targeted EDM campaigns (emails tailored and sent to certain segments of our database) – driving sales on command and increasing the value of our business as an asset. Unfortunately though, the activity of email marketing is underutilised by SSBs. Many of us start a list but don't actively build or maintain it, let alone communicate regularly with those on it, which is as good as having no list at all.

Regular communication does not mean constant communication. In fact, for the majority of SSBs, sending daily, weekly or even fortnightly emails without a clearly defined purpose can do more harm than good. Instead, we need a blend of ***scheduled*** and ***spontaneous communications*** – a structured email sent at periodic intervals of 3–4 months (enough for your business to be remembered and recalled, without becoming an inbox annoyance), supplemented by occasional *special offer* emails to surprise, reward or incentivise. This approach to email marketing provides a good balance. It's enough to demonstrate that you care about your SSB community and to remain top of mind, without contributing to the 'inbox overwhelm' that plagues most email users.

For tips and tricks about email marketing – building a valuable, legal mailing list, spamming regulations and more – refer to Chapter 6 of *Secret Service Marketing*, Lay the Groundwork for Growth.

Mobile Marketing

Mobile marketing refers to the transmission or display of marketing messages on mobile phones and other handheld devices. It can be facilitated in a number of ways, including SMS (short message service), QR code scanning and LBS (location based services) like GPS, Bluetooth or wi-fi messaging. SMS or text messaging is the most popular form of mobile marketing, however an upsurge in geo-targeting and proximity marketing technologies may soon change the game for brick-and-mortar businesses such as cafés, restaurants and salons. Theoretically, with the right systems in place, a café could send notifications to the phones of people who come into a certain proximity,

containing a coupon or the details of an enticing lunch special to generate *hyper-local* awareness and subsequent foot traffic.

Although geo-targeting, proximity marketing and other advanced mobile marketing technologies (like augmented reality and augmented advertising) exist, they are yet to be embraced in a mainstream capacity. Until they are, it's a waste of time and money to prioritise them. As with advances in web design, it's not wise for SSBs to serve as guinea pigs for the latest marketing technologies. Without waiting for the big end of town to forge a path with a new technology until it's socially acceptable and affordable, we're likely to end up extremely disappointed with the return on our investment.

SMS Marketing

The most widely adopted form of mobile marketing is *SMS* – text messages sent directly to individuals' mobile phones via their mobile phone number. This is a powerful means of direct marketing communication, applicable in one way or another to most of us. For the vast majority of SSBs, sending automated reminder messages to customers a day or so before their scheduled appointments (a feature that comes standard in most scheduling systems for service-based businesses) is the single-most valuable way to utilise mobile marketing technology. Confirming your customers' attendance by SMS not only minimises costly no-shows, it builds the perception of your business as a modern, organised and proficient operation.

Using SMS for appointment or booking reminders can pave the way for sending messages of a more promotional nature. Although you never want to bombard customers with promotional messages, the occasional, carefully considered text message promoting a one-time special offer can be extremely effective – not just for filling empty slots in your appointment calendar but to strengthen relationships with customers through proactive communication.

QR Code Campaigns

With 'check-in' programs for COVID-19 contact-tracing, society is more comfortable with QR (Quick Response) code scanning than ever before. As such, it's a good time for SSBs to jump on the scanning bandwagon.

A **QR code** is a 2D pixelated barcode that reveals specific online content to users when scanned with a code scanner (built into the camera app of most smartphones). Often incorporated into the design of promotional materials like flyers or posters, QR codes are not only free to use, they are free to create online via QR code generation websites.

Figure 8: Example of a QR code

QR codes provide prospective customers with a means to access content on a designated webpage at the click of a smartphone button, without having to type a long-winded URL (website address). This portal to rich, related content paves the way for a more immersive service experience and deeper, more emotive connections. For example, a QR code on a 'special of the day' menu could lead to a video of the chef plating up the special dish. Another, on the main menu, could lead to a VIP registration form with a video of the business owner outlining the benefits of completing it. Opportunities like these are available for the vast majority of SSB owners, limited only by our imagination... and now's the time to explore them.

Note that novice QR code users may need help finding the code scanner on their phone for the first time but, once initiated, they're likely to become regular users, due to the sense of curiosity that QR codes have the capacity to invoke.

Snail Mail Marketing

Sending addressed marketing communications via the traditional postal system (aka snail mail), used to be the most common form of direct marketing for SSBs. In comparison to other options, it's now one of the most expensive and difficult to track.

Despite this, *snail mail marketing* is still worthy of consideration and can be cost effective if used strategically. Given society's transition from postal to digital communication, less businesses are using snail mail than ever before but that doesn't mean we should write it off completely. Instead, we can choose to see it as an opportunity to cut through the clutter of modern marketing, reaching customers directly via a medium that's no longer saturated.

If using snail mail marketing, a high-quality, curated mailing list is more essential than ever due to the cost of each letter. Dead letters (those that never reach the intended recipient because of an old address, spelling error, etc) equate to dead money. For this reason, it's better to use snail mail as a means to communicate with, incentivise and reward a specially selected, small group of repeat customers than thousands of individuals at the periphery of your business network.

In addition to a small, high-quality list, carefully crafted communications are essential for successful snail mail marketing. Whether it's a letter introducing a new service or thanking them for their recent patronage, a card acknowledging a special occasion (birthday, Christmas, etc), or any other written correspondence, it should:

- Be **personalised**, with the recipient's name in the greeting line (e.g. 'Dear Susan');
- Highlight the **exclusivity** of the communication (e.g. 'you are one of 100 customers specially selected to receive this letter');
- Contain a **special offer** that's genuinely special;
- Contain a **visual component or article**, such as a brochure, voucher or something more tactile and memorable, such as a magnet or teabag (ensuring it's given context within the written component of the communication).

Snail mail marketing won't generate new customers but, for SSBs with the foresight to recognise and reward customer loyalty, it can be a secondary marketing activity well worth considering.

Viral Marketing

Viral marketing occurs when a piece of online content (usually a blog post, video or captioned image known as a *meme*), gets shared in a virus-like manner by internet users, who find it highly interesting or entertaining and therefore, share-worthy. The content

can go on to be seen by hundreds of thousands, or even millions of people. This viral exposure can be great for business – but for SSBs, it's a long shot. It's virtually impossible to plan a viral marketing campaign because we can't predict what the online world will respond to, nor where our audience will be geographically located.

The greatest chance we have to engage in viral marketing is to create quality content consistently (as per the content marketing section, earlier in the chapter). The more compelling the articles or videos we produce, the greater the chance of one striking a viral chord.

If the long haul approach to viral marketing doesn't appeal to you, try engaging in other forms of guerrilla marketing with a camera rolling nearby. Many viral video sensations are created when a video camera happens to be filming in the right place, at the right time. Guerrilla marketing (such as a street marketing stunt – explained next) can set the scene for that. If any amusing incidents or interactions are captured, they can be posted online, shared with personal and professional networks and the chips of viral marketing left to fall where they may. Bear in mind, however, that even if a video does gain traction, there's no guarantee it will benefit your business' bottom line.

Street Marketing – Free or Low Cost

Street marketing aims to draw attention to a brand or business by engaging passers-by in a public place such as a footpath, event, shopping centre, park or beach. Examples of street marketing include handing out

coupons or samples in a nearby mall, dressing up in a costume to wave a sign in view of passing traffic, executing coordinated stunts (such as a flash mob dance) or featuring amusing quotes or jokes on an outdoor message board.

Street marketing is an excellent way to add depth and personality to a brand on a tight budget. With a little initiative and creativity, it's possible to make your business more personable and memorable and help it stand out from similar service providers in your local area.

Before embarking on a street marketing activity, be sure to check for applicable rules and regulations. Look up the website of your national regulatory body (such as the ACCC in Australia) for protocols surrounding the approach of individuals in the street. Also check with your local council, as not all street marketing activities are permitted in all areas.

————————

Surviving on Low Cost Activities Alone

Many of us have been conditioned to think we need to spend a lot of money on marketing to be taken seriously or generate lasting momentum. That's no longer the case. In this day and age, with the tools and technologies at our disposal, it's well and truly possible for SSBs to thrive with a suite of free or low-cost activities from the survival, no-brainer and cheap but challenging categories. To achieve this coveted marketing scenario however, five things are a must.

1. **An interest in marketing and technology** – While many low-cost marketing activities can be delegated, outsourced

or automated (online review management and SEO, for example), others (such as content marketing and social media activity) don't have the same impact if they're not closely overseen or actioned by the SSB owner. They require the owner's authenticity and expertise to cut through and connect. That's why, before selecting the more challenging of marketing activities, it's important to be honest about your level of interest in them, as well as your desire to acquire and hone the necessary technical skills. None of these activities are rocket science, but there is usually a steep learning curve and an ongoing commitment of time and energy.

2. **Marketing tools** – As explained at the start of the book, marketing activity alone isn't enough. Activities generate awareness and attention but it's our marketing tools – particularly a website – that boost the chances of potential customers taking action, becoming identified prospects (leads) and converting into paying customers (sales). A detailed rundown on marketing tools is provided in Chapter 6.

3. **Respect** – No matter what activities you employ, respect for your audience is essential. This means considering your target market and customers as people, not walking wallets; acting and communicating with integrity, prioritising the quality of your communications over the quantity, and remembering that your SSB exists to serve those who support you, not to annoy, bore or bombard them with constant promotional offers.

4. **Patience** – Patience is part and parcel of low-cost marketing. Some activities, such as outbound telemarketing, can reap fairly swift rewards. Others, like content marketing and social media activity, take time to gain traction. Don't

expect to alter the course of business history overnight. Good things take time.

Patience is also required to nurture leads and contacts. Don't disregard those who aren't fulfilling the criteria to be considered a viable lead right now. Play your cards right and they'll become tomorrow's leads and sales (be it next month, next year or whenever the need for your service arises). A mailing list is key to this, paving the way for the use of direct marketing (by email, phone and/or mail) to keep the lines of communication open.

5. **Perseverance** – If a marketing campaign (consisting of a social media post and EDM, for example) fails to generate the desired response, it doesn't mean the activities (social media activity and email marketing) aren't worth pursuing. In most cases, failure indicates that a message hasn't resonated with its audience – the offer, copywriting, call-to-action or visual presentation are off track due to a misunderstanding of the target market's needs. The only way to determine if certain marketing activities have the capacity to work for you is to persevere – tweaking the messages over time and monitoring the results. Within a matter of months, you're sure to look back on your first attempt, laugh at how unprofessional it looks and be proud of how far you've come.

CHAPTER 5.

UPPER END ACTIVITIES

If you lack the time or willpower for survival, no-brainer and cheap but challenging activities, there's no alternative but to splash out some cash. Without a willingness to DIY, upper end marketing activities – including advertising – become the only option.

As many advertising sales reps would gladly attest, the benefit of paying for ads is that fresh eyes or ears *will* see or hear about your business. But fresh eyes and ears are no guarantee of leads and sales. In not realising this, many of us go wrong – spending a fortune on individual, ad hoc marketing activities under the false belief that they'll catapult our business to success. Invariably they don't and, instead of the upsurge in sales we're expecting, we're left feeling disappointed and disillusioned, scrambling to replenish our bank balance.

This is not to suggest that upper end activities aren't worthwhile. They certainly can be but, to generate a return on investment, we must be strategic in their selection and implementation. The first step toward this is becoming familiar with the depth and breadth of upper end activities available. TV, radio and print ads tend to spring to mind when we think of big-ticket marketing activities but these comprise just one of many options, as listed below.

Figure 9: Upper End Activities

Marketing Type	Marketing Activity (Opportunity)
Handshake Marketing	• Expos and Trade Shows
e3 Marketing	• Online Directories – Paid Listings • Group Buying (Daily Deal) Website Campaigns
Search Engine Marketing	• Search Engine Optimisation – Outsourced • Search Engine Advertising
Social Media Marketing	• Social Media Advertising
Local Area Marketing	• Community Facility Advertising – Paid • Resident Distribution Advertising – Paid
Guerrilla Marketing	• Street Marketing – High Cost
Mass Marketing	• Mainstream Media Advertising

I avoid recommending upper end activities to SSB owners unless a particularly promising opportunity exists. By this, I mean an opportunity to attract the attention of a clearly defined target market, in person or via advertising communications, at a fair and feasible price. These opportunities rarely land in our lap (and if they do, it's wise to retain a healthy sense of scepticism until they're thoroughly assessed, as explained in Chapter 7). Instead, they need to be strategically sought out by getting a firm grasp of the needs, interests and habits of the target market: what they read and watch, events they attend, who they follow on social media, etc to determine what paid activities could reach them.

For most SSBs, it's possible to avoid upper end options by striking the right blend of no-brainer and cheap but challenging activities, but that's not always ideal. Sometimes, particularly in highly competitive industries or markets, the time, effort and skill required to gain traction with low-cost activities is too much and an ongoing investment in a carefully selected big-ticket activity can be a wiser option. Other times, in less competitive situations, not being open to upper end activities can leave profitable marketing opportunities on the table.

The point is, no matter what service you provide or how competitive your industry is, upper end activities are worth considering – even for those of us who consider ourselves puritanical Secret Service Marketers. The Secret Service approach is about getting the biggest bang for your marketing buck, *not* about never spending a cent.

With that in mind, let's take a look at each upper end activity, starting with the highest cost means of handshake marketing.

Expos & Trade Shows

Expos and trade shows are events at which the goods and services of many businesses – in the same industry or with a similar target market – are exhibited via temporary stands in a hall or pavilion. For the organisers of these events, the aim is to bring a pool of buyers with a particular interest together with a pool of applicable sellers to interact and transact, profiting via exhibition fees and/or ticket sales.

Consumer expos and trade shows are geared for consumer markets (B2C) – individuals as opposed to businesses. They can be general in nature or tailored around a particular industry or target market. *Industry* expos and trade shows are geared for business markets (B2B), designed to attract business representatives or professionals in a certain industry. A boat cleaning business may exhibit at The Boat Show, a maternity masseuse at The Pregnancy, Babies & Children's Expo or a commercial builder, specialising in dental office fitouts, at a dental trade show.

Exhibiting at an expo or trade show can be useful for SSBs. It provides a unique opportunity to meet face-to-face with hundreds or thousands of service seekers, create brand awareness and generate leads and sales.

But not all participating businesses benefit financially from these events. Hiring a stand at an expo or trade show can cost thousands of dollars, without factoring in the cost of stand staging, signage, promotional materials, staffing, nor indirect planning, preparation and transportation costs. Depending on the price point of the showcased goods or services and the number of similar vendors participating in the event, it can be difficult to cover the costs of being involved. While it can prove highly beneficial and an activity to repeat year after year, participating in an expo or trade show can, through no fault of your own, end in regret. That's why, instead of leaving it to chance, it's crucial to make an informed decision. This means doing your due diligence – objectively crunching the numbers and considering certain qualitative factors, presented in Chapter 7.

If your investigations check out and you book a stand, the most crucial aspect of planning for an expo or trade show is deciding what you want out of it. The priority could be to collect leads or grow your mailing list, make on-the-spot sales or take bookings for the delivery of a particular service – whatever has the capacity for the most tangible, measurable outcome. Once this has been determined, everything else should be geared to support it; the stand, promotional offers and marketing materials all tailored to encourage the action you want potential customers to take. This could include signs and brochures to promote a certain service or offer, an exclusive 'expo only' package or bonus, or entry into a draw in exchange for attendees' business cards, for example. Deciding upon and executing these tactics with precision is key to making the most of an opportunity to exhibit at any event, no matter how much you've paid to be there.

Online Directories – Paid Listings

Most online business directories (except not-for-profit directories and those provided by search engines) present an option to upgrade from a free to a paid listing. The benefits of upgrading are typically promoted as: 1) greater exposure on the directory site, 2) greater exposure in search engines, and 3) a more comprehensive, enticing listing – all equating to higher visibility and more leads. While these benefits can come to fruition, paid directory listings can also be a waste of money, particularly if results aren't tracked and the listing goes on being mindlessly renewed year after year.

As with any paid marketing activity, it's important to do your homework before upgrading to a paid listing on an online directory. Specific questions to ask the directory's sales rep include:

- How many searches per month are performed for my service, in my local region, on the directory site itself? This question shines a light on how actively the site is used as an 'on-page' search directory, by service seekers of relevance to your business. Be sure to ask for visual proof of this statistic and study it carefully.

- What combinations of services and suburbs/regions would users need to search for specifically, for my business listing to rank first or second in your directory search results? If the answer is too specific, e.g. 'commercial builder Ascot Park' (as opposed to commercial builder Adelaide)... forget it.

- What tracking mechanisms do you have in place to demonstrate how many leads are coming to me directly from your site?

- Will I be locked into a contract? If so, for how long?

- If I take out a paid listing, where will my business listing rank amongst my competitors listings, for general service/location searches performed: 1) on the directory site, and 2) on Google? If the rep responds promisingly, ask how they can guarantee it.

- Where will I stand if we are a few months into the contract and my listing is not ranking well and/or not driving any leads?

As with free listings, paid listings on online directory sites can rarely be relied on as a primary marketing activity. They are a supporting activity, at best, and should be prioritised and assessed accordingly.

Group Buying (Daily Deal) Website Campaigns

Group buying websites promote and sell bulk quantities of goods and services on behalf of businesses at significantly reduced prices, charging a fee or commission for the privilege. These sites – Groupon, Scoopon, Spreets, LivingSocial and the like, commonly referred to as daily deal sites – can be a good medium for SSBs to create a pool of new customers... *if* the campaign is carefully thought out, managed well and viewed as a marketing investment, not a money-spinner. Otherwise it can be disastrous; depleting your business' bank balance along with its reputation.

The main reason to consider offering a service at a discounted rate through a group buying site is to generate exposure and resultant 'bums on seats'. If considered and executed strategically, this can be a highly beneficial strategy, providing a handy cash flow boost during off-peak or quiet periods, for example. The turnover generated by group buying campaigns is typically low-profit, but that's okay. As long as the campaign is approached in a realistic, healthy way and facilitated well, it has the capacity to generate high-profit turnover into the future through repeat patronage and word of mouth.

Disaster stems from assuming a group buying campaign is the answer to your marketing prayers or the key to entrepreneurial fame and fortune. For the record, it's neither. Group buying campaigns are geared to generate new customers and sales turnover. To translate into repeat customers and healthy profits, the lack of profit on the initial transaction needs to be considered a cost of the activity itself. This cost is one to be accepted and absorbed, not offset by squeezing extra money out of campaign customers on the day their service is delivered.

The most important things to remember when embarking on a group buying campaign are:

1. **Create a high value package** – The appeal and perceived value of any promotional offer hinges on how it's packaged and presented. With a group buying offer, it can be enhanced by throwing in extra goods, services or benefits (such as a complimentary tea or coffee on arrival, a bonus head massage with a hair cut/colour, etc) – things that can be included with minimal extra cost that transform the service into an *experience* for the customer. A restaurant could add a bottle of wine to a meal deal for example, having sourced a supply of quality cleanskin wines at $4 a bottle – a small cost that adds significantly to the perceived value of the offer.

2. **Cover costs** – As obvious as it might sound, it's vital to ensure the discounted price of a group buying deal covers the costs incurred to promote and deliver it (including the cost of goods sold, group buying campaign fees/commissions and any other expenses). The only exception to this rule is if you're willing and able to make a loss on the promotion, as a strategic marketing move.

3. **Avoid the hard sell** – Most group buying customers take offers at face value, not expecting to be upsold, sideswiped or pressured to return at full price. Attempting to squeeze more money out of them than they've already invested can undermine the entire experience and put a nail in the coffin of the buyer/seller relationship. It's far more effective to take a 'softly, softly' approach to group buying transactions

– taking the time to build rapport before gently suggesting complementary goods or additional services (if applicable) with no talk of price unless the customer initiates it.

4. **Treat campaign customers as VIPs** – One of the most common reasons group buying customers don't return to a business as full-paying customers is because they feel judged for being 'cheap', having been treated by staff as second-class citizens. For group buying campaigns to result in repeat patronage and positive word of mouth, customers must be treated as VIPs; appreciated and pandered to, as much as full-paying customers, if not more. The aim of the group buying game is to leave them so delighted with the overall experience that they want to come back or, at the very least, tell their friends.

Done right, and for the right reasons, group buying campaigns can be extremely beneficial. Planned with purpose, precision and a commitment to go above and beyond to impress every customer (without pressuring them to spend more than they already have), group buying campaigns have the capacity to take an SSB to a new level of growth and profitability and, as such, are well worth investigating.

Search Engine Optimisation – Outsourced

Presented in Chapter 3, do-it-yourself search engine optimisation (SEO) is a no-brainer activity but it's not suitable for everyone. For those who aren't used to delving into the back-end of a website, it can be overwhelming and

time-consuming. And even the more website-savvy of us can find the delay between doing SEO work and seeing pagerank improvements frustrating. For many business owners, DIY SEO can prove too great a challenge. And if so... then what?

Avoiding SEO is not the answer. That would mean ignoring one of the most powerful marketing opportunities of our time – the opportunity to rank well on Google. Fortunately, becoming an SEO superhero or burying our head in the sand are not our only options. If funds allow, an SEO expert can be engaged to sweet-talk the search engines for us.

Of all upper end marketing activities, outsourcing the SEO function can be one of the most beneficial. But, depending who you engage and for how long, it can be very expensive. If you're not careful, outsourcing SEO can prove more frustrating and infinitely more costly than a failed attempt at doing it yourself. This is due to the nature of the search engine marketing industry – an industry littered with cowboys, who promise the world but don't have the capacity or conscientiousness to deliver.

Of the SEO providers I've worked with, I had the best experiences with a freelancer hired on the outsourcing platform Upwork. I identified Thomas (from Western Europe) as a suitable candidate, having studied his profile and portfolio amongst a plethora of others. Although his hourly rate was much higher than most, he stood out as a genuine expert. I posted an 'invitation only' job, invited him to apply and we engaged in preliminary discussions. Thomas was open to negotiation and upfront about outsourcing part of the work offshore. Having worked with agencies who'd sought to hide the fact that they were outsourcing some, if not all, of the work, I found Thomas' transparency refreshing and decided to give him a go.

Thomas quickly became my go-to guy for all things SEO. I had no complaints, only compliments. He was highly invested in his work and managed his subcontractors impeccably. He communicated clearly, was caring, responsible and accountable, did thorough research, was marketing-minded, offered flexibility in the length and scope of our contracts and most importantly, got results. Of course, it would be silly to deduce from this that individual SEO freelancers are always better than agencies – obviously there's good and bad in both, and everyone's experience will be different. But, for me, one attempt at hiring an SEO freelancer on Upwork proved infinitely more successful than multiple attempts at hiring local agencies. Take from that what you will.

Before outsourcing your SEO, note that if using Upwork or any outsourcing platform with the intention of getting a cheap deal, it will almost certainly lead to disappointment. For the attention to detail required for SEO to work as intended, particularly in a competitive market, expect to pay a reasonable price.

That said, there is a way to control the cost of SEO, born from the fact that (contrary to common belief) the effects of quality SEO are residual. Your Google ranking won't suddenly plummet if an SEO specialist stops working on your website. It may drop a little over time as the Google algorithm changes but it won't happen overnight. Knowing this can be a gamechanger; giving you the freedom to be more strategic in your approach to outsourcing SEO.

Because the effects of SEO are residual, it can be done periodically. Rather than engaging an SEO provider on an ongoing basis, or for as long as financially feasible, you can elect to engage them for a kick-off contract of 6–10 months (depending on the level of competition in your field and region of service), followed by periodic stints of 3–6 months, every year or two. A periodic approach to SEO can help your business enjoy the best of both worlds – remaining visible and competitive in search engine listings and saving a fortune on ongoing fees.

Engaging an SEO provider for a substantial length of time to begin with (the kick-off contract), is essential. When it's never been done before, SEO can take several months to have a noticeable effect on search engine rankings and resultant website traffic, so it's necessary to commit for a minimum of 6 months. Once traction has been gained and maintained for a couple of months, the brakes can be put on – ceasing optimisation activity but continuing to monitor rankings and results.

A year or two down the track it can be ramped up again, with the same SEO provider or a new one. Engaging a different provider can be risky but rewarding; bringing new knowledge, skills and experience to the table, along with fresh eyes to spot overlooked SEO opportunities.

No matter whether you're outsourcing SEO for the first time or the tenth, with the same provider or a new one, it's important to remain vigilant and involved. SEO work isn't easy to track or trace, which means months can fly by with no work being done on your site, and you would never know. To reduce the risk of this, you're well within your rights to ask the provider to: 1) outline the SEO tasks they're planning to undertake at the beginning of each month, 2) report back at the end of the month with the progress that's been made, and 3) provide independent pagerank reports every month or quarter showing the cumulative effects of their work. Although not a foolproof plan, this will keep lines of communication open, encourage accountability and reinforce the expectation of progress and results.

Search Engine Advertising

Beyond the opportunity to rank higher in
organic listings through search engine optimisation, search engines give businesses
the opportunity to pay for advertising
space. For a fee, they will display ads in the
'Sponsored Links' section of search results and elsewhere online
(via the Google Display Network, for example). This opportunity
is referred to as *search engine advertising (SEA)*.

SEA has a unique cost structure. Campaigns can be set up as:

- *Cost-per-click (CPC)* – Charged each time a user clicks an ad;
- *Cost-per-thousand impressions (CPM)* – Charged every
  1000 times an ad is displayed, whether users engage with
  it or not;
- *Cost-per-view (CPV)* – Charged each time an ad is viewed
  (typically only available for video ads).

Determining the most cost effective billing option for your
business is a matter of trial and error, but don't let that deter
you from giving it a go. Whether you opt for CPC or CPM, the
total amount payable at the end of a billing period is likely to
be similar. That's because, although CPC and CPM rates are
different, they both stem from the level of competition for
the search terms you want your ads to appear for. The cost of
ads displayed in response to searches for 'hairdresser London'
would be substantially higher than those for 'hairdresser Broken
Hill', for example. It's all relative.

SEA is often misleadingly labelled *search engine marketing (SEM)*
by digital marketing companies seeking to muddy the waters
between SEO and SEA. If hiring a company to undertake SEM, it's
SEA in disguise; they will coordinate an SEA campaign and charge

hundreds or thousands of dollars in campaign management fees for the privilege. If you pay for SEM under the assumption that it's SEO, you'll be sorely disappointed because, unlike SEO, SEA has no residual benefit. If you stop paying, your ads stop displaying.

SEO not only has longer lasting benefits, it is more powerful than SEA. Research shows that 15% of all website visits come from clicks on paid search engine ads, while 53% come from clicks on organic search engine listings (generated through SEO).[8] This indicates that searchers prefer organic search listings over paid ones. Searchers aren't silly – they realise that anyone can pay for an ad but a decent organic ranking has to be earned. For this and many other reasons, I rarely recommend SEA as a primary marketing activity for SSBs, opting for those that garner more respect and have longer term benefits.

Although it's not my cup of tea, many service businesses rely on SEA to be found online. It *can* work and there are many SEA opportunities to explore without breaking the bank – particularly if you're prepared to create and run campaigns yourself, or engage a savvy, fairly-priced freelancer to do it for you.

For SSBs, the greatest SEA opportunities typically involve keyword research and campaign types, as explained below.

Keyword Opportunities

A vital part of search engine marketing is determining what keywords and phrases potential customers are entering into search engines, specific to the goods or services to be promoted. This is integral to SEO but equally as important for SEA. It's often possible to tap into a juicy stream of traffic by identifying 'long tail keywords' overlooked by competitors, and crafting cost effective SEA campaigns around them.

As with SEO, keyword research can be carried out using a free online tool called Google Keyword Planner. Accessed via the Google AdWords platform (where SEA campaigns are created and managed), Keyword Planner provides a means to research the monthly volume of searches for particular keywords or phrases, within a defined geographic location. This is a fascinating exercise for any business owner – those contemplating SEA or not. It reveals the level of competition for particular search terms, suggestions for alternative keywords and how much an Adwords campaign might cost; insights key to determining the feasibility of SEA and building a strong campaign.

Campaign Opportunities

Search engine ads take different forms depending on the campaign type selected. For SSBs, the three main types are:

- **Text advertising** – Often preceded by the word 'Ad' or the heading 'Sponsored Links', text ads are short, word-only line ads (like classified ads of old) that appear at the top and side of the search engine results page (SERP). Text ads are the most common form of paid online advertising and the type most familiar to SSB owners. If you've dabbled with SEA, it was probably with text ads.

- **Display advertising** – A step up from text ads, display ads typically contain an image, video, animation and/or audio for greater advertising impact. Formats include:

    - **Basic ads** – Square or rectangular ads positioned within a page of content;

    - **Floating banners** – Ads that travel across the screen or float above a website's content;

- **Wallpapers** – Ads that fill the background of a website;
- **Popups** – Ads that appear in a new window, in front of a website's content.

Unlike text ads, display ads are presented on third party websites. They can be set to display on sites with a certain theme or user demographic, or more broadly, on unrelated sites.

Display ads cost less per click than text ads but there's a reason for that... they tend to be less effective. Internet users can be bombarded with hundreds of ads in a single browsing session. They are adept at tuning ads out – particularly ones that are highly visual and therefore, obvious as ads. For this reason, display ads tend not to perform as well as text ads and it can be difficult to gain traction with them – unless they're used in conjunction with a third campaign type: *remarketing*.

- **Remarketing** – Taking effectiveness and cost into consideration, remarketing offers the single greatest SEA opportunity for SSBs. It involves delivering display ads *only* to internet users who have visited a business' website or watched its YouTube videos.

Remarketing campaigns work through the use of cookies. Once set up, the computers of those who visit a business' website or YouTube videos are digitally tagged with a cookie, triggering ads to appear to them in ensuing days, weeks and months while they browse other sites on the internet. Having previously come across the business' content, they're likely to recognise the brand and be receptive to its advertising messages. As ads continue to appear, familiarity builds – increasing the likelihood of them taking action.

Remarketing is an efficient way to satisfy the Rule of Seven or *seven touches* theory – an old marketing adage attributed to marketer Dr. Jeffrey Lant.[9] Lant claimed that to penetrate buyer consciousness, businesses need to contact or communicate with them a minimum of seven times in an 18-month period.

Given the dynamic environment businesses exist in today, seven touches is considered a major understatement by modern marketers in big business. However, the rule is still applicable to SSBs with a Lead Machine, who have the power to generate conversions with far fewer touches. Using remarketing, it's possible to amplify the effectiveness of an SSB website by presenting ads to visitors six times (or more) in the following days, weeks and months – catching as many of those who slip through the site's conversion cracks as possible.

As it's so highly targeted, remarketing is usually inexpensive and, if done right, can be much more effective than text ads. It has the power to dramatically increase online conversions by reminding those who've shown an interest in your goods or services that your business exists and is ready to serve them. If they aren't interested in engaging your services, they won't click the ads, and if they don't click the ads, you don't pay. So there's nothing to lose by putting a remarketing campaign in place.

While SEA agencies can be hired to facilitate text, display and remarketing ad campaigns, you *can* do it yourself – avoiding hefty campaign management fees. Setting up an SEA campaign has a steep learning curve (arguably steeper than SEO) but for those who are so inclined, it can be a rewarding side project with a direct and measurable return.

Social Media Advertising

Social media advertising is similar to search engine advertising but, instead of the search engine results page or a random website, ads are presented to users via their social networking feed or interface. Advertising via an applicable social media platform – such as Facebook, Instagram, YouTube, LinkedIn, TikTok, X or Pinterest – can be worthwhile and cost effective for SSBs, due to the ability to target an audience with intricate precision. Campaigns can be geared to serve ads to individuals who meet highly specific criteria: age, gender, location, relationship status, life stage, personal and professional interests, online behaviours and more.

Like with SEA, there are various types of social media advertising. These range from promoted posts and pages to display or video ad campaigns. Most social media platforms have a range of pricing and ad delivery options, including remarketing – which can be a highly effective option, just as it is with SEA.

Not all social media platforms are applicable to all businesses. LinkedIn, Facebook or YouTube are often used for business-to-business (B2B) advertising, and Facebook, Instagram, YouTube, TikTok, X, Pinterest and others, for business-to-consumer (B2C) advertising, however there's no hard and fast rule. Each platform provides a different user experience, has its own intricacies at the front and back end and provides a unique suite of advertising opportunities. As such, each needs to be assessed for the opportunities it offers and how well it aligns with a business' objectives and target market. Using Google to research who certain platforms are used by and what kinds of businesses find success with them (including the advertising strategies they use) is an excellent place to start.

Community Facility Advertising – Paid

As explained in Chapter 3, some community facility advertising opportunities are available for free, while others come at a price. Wherever the local community publicly convenes, paid advertising opportunities can usually be found. Examples include:

- **Shopping centres** – Leased mall stands or pop-up shops/displays;
- **Sports grounds** – Advertorial signage on fences and branding on player uniforms, as part of a sports team sponsorship package;
- **Supermarkets** – Ads/coupons on the back of supermarket dockets (through programs such as Shopa Docket);
- **Cinemas** – Big screen advertisements (multimedia or a static image with an accompanying voiceover).

Paid community facility advertising works in a similar way to mainstream media advertising – through repeat brand exposure – but on a smaller geographic scale. Its reach is contained to those who frequent local facilities.

Community facility advertising can be a worthwhile investment for SSBs, particularly when approached as a medium- to long-term strategy. Unlike other forms of advertising, community facility advertising demonstrates an active affiliation with the local community. The perception and effect of this affiliation compounds over time, which means businesses need to be in it for the long haul to reap the full effect. It takes multiple exposures over an extended period of time to penetrate the minds of those frequenting a local facility, so, if you can't afford to commit to a community facility advertising opportunity on an ongoing basis, you might want to give it a miss.

Resident Distribution Advertising – Paid

Among the no-brainers presented in Chapter 3, we covered DIY resident distribution advertising – the low-cost activity of delivering promotional materials such as flyers to homes or businesses in a designated area. For those of us who like the idea of promoting our services to a geographically targeted group of residents but lack the time or inclination to walk the streets ourselves, an intermediary or 'middleman' can be paid to bridge the gap.

Intermediaries for resident distribution advertising come in two forms:

1. **Local publications** – Community newspapers and regional phone directories delivered to local residents for free, funded by the sale of advertising space in each edition;

2. **Brochure distribution agencies** – Businesses that collate
   and deliver brochures and catalogues to householders on
   behalf of individual advertisers.

Advertising in local newspapers via display or classified ads
proves cost effective for many service providers – personal,
professional, medical and trade services to name a few. As
with community facility advertising however, consistency and
longevity is key. One or two ads in the local rag will do little
for your bottom line – in fact, the cost of the ads is likely to
deplete it. Committing to advertise every alternate week for
three months or more is a wiser approach, giving the activity
time to take effect. While months of biweekly ads cost more
than a spasmodic burst of one or two, it paves the way for the
repeat exposure required to build salience and trust.

Printed phone directories such as the White and Yellow Pages
do still exist, although they're much thinner and lighter than
they once were. Some service seekers do still use them – they
can be an effective means of advertising to older people, for
example. However, when considering a listing or more prominent display ad in a regional directory, it's crucial to consider
not just the applicability of the distribution area, but who uses it
within that area and for what. Without doing this groundwork,
advertising in a regional directory can prove futile.

Distribution of brochures and catalogues to letterboxes is
facilitated by agencies such as IVE Group (formerly Salmat)
or Bell Print in Australia. The services of large distribution
agencies are most commonly utilised by large goods-based
businesses such as supermarkets and department stores but
scores of smaller agencies exist too, servicing businesses of all

types and sizes, including SSBs. Engaging a distribution agency to deliver a flyer or menu to a few thousand householders can be surprisingly affordable, however it can get quite expensive over large regions; printing and distribution costs soon add up.

Whether a paid letterbox drop proves cost effective or not comes down to its *response rate* – how many residents take action as a result of receiving the flyer. If response rates are low (which they often are for services), a large campaign probably won't prove feasible. For this reason, it's wise to test the waters with a small print/distribution run of one or two thousand residents first – following the flyer design tips provided in the DIY resident distribution section of Chapter 3 – before rolling it out over a larger area.

Street Marketing – High Cost

As introduced in Chapter 4, street marketing for SSB owners is usually cheap and cheerful; handing out coupons or cupcakes, or donning a costume to attract the attention of passers by. However, there are other, more expensive options – limited only by your imagination and budget.

High-end forms of street marketing include experiential booths, interactive advertisements or displays, branded sporting events and other public spectacles. While activities such as these have the capacity to generate mass exposure, they are an extravagance – out of reach for the vast majority of SSBs.

Even if a street marketing opportunity is affordable, it won't necessarily be impactful. Like with viral marketing, it's best if there's a strong correlation between the business' offering, brand or purpose and the experience or event being facilitated, such as Red Bull Energy Drinks' sponsorship of extreme sporting events.

For SSBs, the best way to benefit from upper end street marketing activities is to 'hitch a ride'... investing in activities coordinated by wealthier organisations or local community groups. Constructing a float to participate in an annual community Christmas pageant (ensuring the float has some visual significance to the goods or services your business offers) is an example of a solid street marketing strategy. Carefully considered street marketing activities such as this can have subtle but incremental benefits – solidifying an SSB's position as a pillar of the local community, while generating brand exposure and PR opportunities year after year.

Mainstream Media Advertising

Mainstream media advertising refers to commercials on television or radio, ads in print media (state or national newspapers/magazines) and/or large-scale outdoor advertising, such as billboards or ads on public transport. Commonly called traditional or mass advertising, mainstream media advertising works through exposure of a brand to the general public, en masse. It was long considered the holy grail of marketing activities – something most SSB owners could only dream of, due to the cost of creating and running an effective campaign.

Times have changed, however, and so too has the use of mainstream media by the general public. Far fewer consumers embrace traditional media and the advertising that goes with it – opting for user-driven digital media instead. This shift has had an enormous impact on the perception of, and demand for, mainstream media advertising by corporate advertisers, who are allocating more resources to online marketing and less to the four traditional offline mediums of TV, radio, print and outdoor.

Reduced demand for ad spots in mainstream media has changed the advertising game, cultivating opportunities for SSBs. With less competition for ads, businesses of all sizes are more likely to be able to negotiate with media outlets on terms such as ad rate or campaign duration. For SSBs, a little negotiation can go a long way, making a previously unattainable advertising opportunity feasible. Financially, there is no better time for SSBs to dip a toe in the water of mass marketing. That said, those waters can be choppy.

For SSBs, mainstream media advertising tends to be 'hit or miss'. Even when mainstream media was booming, I'd often hear tales of small businesses investing in expensive advertisements in the hope of taking their business to the next level. Unfortunately, most of these stories ended with disappointment. The ads usually resulted in little new business unless a highly competitive financial incentive (price-based reward or discount) was offered to prospective customers. Even then, the results were short-lived, with residual cash flow or customer relations issues offsetting the perceived success of the campaign, and no impact on the business' bottom line beyond the come-down of the promotion.

That's not to say mainstream media advertising can't work or isn't worth a try. It can be a great option to explore if:

- The medium of advertising you're considering has a strong, relevant audience that corresponds with your target market;
- You are logistically prepared for a favourable response, equipped with the marketing tools to convert interested viewers/listeners/readers into tangible leads;
- You have other, more targeted marketing activities in place so you're not relying on it alone, or resorting to it out of desperation;
- You're able to strike a fair deal with the media outlet – one you can afford as a medium to long-term branding activity, not just a one-off promotional exercise.

If any of these boxes aren't ticked, it's better to steer clear of mainstream media – focusing on the more strategic, affordable activities in your arsenal until you're in a strong enough position to bear the brunt of a failed campaign.

As a rule of thumb for selecting a paid marketing activity: the more targetable it is, the better – hence, a shift in focus from mainstream to digital advertising. Marketers have realised that, unlike mainstream methods, the internet provides a more efficient way of reaching an audience. It allows us to aim at and hit our target market with a high degree of accuracy, as opposed to the loose, scattergun approach of mainstream media advertising. Online, we can narrow the reach of our marketing message to people located in a certain region and/or with a highly specific demographic profile, resulting in a higher return on investment.

That said, just because the demand for mainstream media advertising has fallen, it doesn't mean it's not worth considering. When businesses steer towards the latest marketing trend, an empty space is left behind. If you're smart and strategic about it (ensuring an ample proportion of your target market still uses the medium you're considering), you can use this to your advantage; sweeping in to secure good deals that arise from reduced competition for ad space. Other, more targetable, offline activities – such as trade shows and resident distribution advertising – can present similar opportunities too, so never dismiss an activity solely on the basis of price. Keep in touch with upper end advertising reps and you just might bag a bargain.

Ready or Not?

No paid marketing activity should be agreed to impulsively or actioned flippantly – especially an expensive one. The more an activity costs, the more revenue it needs to generate to break even, so the higher the risk involved. Risk is not a bad thing (in fact, it's par for the entrepreneurial course) but it does need to be calculated. Without carefully considering the risk of an expensive activity before signing up for it, we're not only gambling with our business' marketing budget... we may be gambling with its future.

To minimise the risk of a paid marketing activity, there are two things to do before committing. The first is to use an objective process to assess the opportunity. Without this, we risk making a business decision based on hope or assumption alone. Such decisions rarely end well.

The second is to have a tried and tested suite of ***marketing tools*** in place, ready to capitalise on the awareness and interest the activity generates. Without the right tools, we risk flushing the time, effort and money we invest on the activity down the drain by not having the mechanisms in place to convert intangible interest into identifiable leads.

So, before discovering how to assess opportunities and decide what marketing activities to implement, let's turn our attention to marketing tools – what they are and which ones are the most crucial to SSB success.

CHAPTER 6.

THE SECRET SERVICE SIX

While some marketing activities can be effective in isolation (typically survival activities), most require the active support of one or more marketing tools to unleash their performance power.

Marketing tools are physical or digital apparatus geared to capitalise on the attention induced by marketing activity. There are six tools in the Secret Service arsenal:

1. A Lead Machine (website geared to drive leads)
2. A sales kit
3. Automated phone messages
4. Email signatures and canned responses
5. Business cards
6. Promotional products

Of these six tools, the aim of the first four is to engage, educate and inspire *immediate* action from prospective customers. The last two (business cards and promotional products) serve better as reminder mechanisms – helping a business stay in prospects' minds to prompt action at some point *in the future*.

Marketing activities and marketing tools (aka the *Secret Service Six*) need each other. They are interdependent and intrinsically linked. Focusing on one over the other (like many of us do when building a website – expecting leads to start rolling in without determining where the traffic necessary for that to happen will come from) is the equivalent of SSB self-sabotage. Without marketing tools, we undermine the effectiveness of our marketing activity and without marketing activity, we undermine the effectiveness of our marketing tools. So, we need both.

When it comes to organising and implementing our marketing arsenal however, tools take priority. Marketing tools are the key to capitalising on marketing activity, so it's ideal that they be in place before an activity commences, or as soon as possible after recognising they are missing.

In order of importance, a rundown of the Secret Service Six (including where to find further information, if applicable) is provided below.

A Lead Machine (website geared to drive leads)

While all six marketing tools are important, one – a Lead Machine – stands head and shoulders above the rest, surpassing all others in its ability to change the game for a struggling SSB.

As mentioned previously – and down to the finest detail in *The Secret Service Website Formula* – a Lead Machine is a website designed to convert traffic into leads. It's also the single greatest marketing investment an SSB owner can make. Having a well-functioning Lead Machine is the only way we can rely on no-brainer marketing activities to organically acquire new customers. Without it, we have to spend much more time or money to get anywhere near the same result.

A Sales Kit

The tools and techniques used to present an offer to a prospective customer in a sales meeting go a long way to determining whether they'll convert into paying clients. For some SSBs, the sales meeting takes the form of a phone call – answering a few simple questions, providing reassurance and booking an appointment. For others, it's a lengthy face-to-face consultation – guiding a prospect through a structured sales presentation, or introducing a menu and a set of daily specials. Whatever the sales process that's most appropriate for our business, we mustn't skimp on it; taking the time to consider the structure of our sales meetings and to develop a suite of supporting resources called a *sales kit*. A comprehensive, well-considered sales kit equips us to present our goods or services in the best possible light. It helps ensure everything that needs to be covered in a sales meeting gets covered; freeing us to be the most authentic, consistent and high-performing salesperson we can be.

For a guide to overhaul your sales process and supporting materials, refer to Chapters 17 and 18 of *Secret Service Marketing* – Make the Most of Fresh Leads and Supercharge your Sales Meetings.

Automated Phone Messages

As explained in the inbound telemarketing section of Chapter 2, the phone is a pivotal point of contact between service seekers and an SSB, but one that many of us take for granted. To that end, the following scenarios are common in small business:

- Calls going unanswered without giving potential customers the opportunity to leave a message;
- Calls not being returned quickly, or worse, not being returned at all;
- Callers being spoken to coldly or bluntly – as if they are an inconvenience;
- Callers being put on hold – left listening to mind-numbing music or empty silence, often wondering if the call has been disconnected.

To minimise undesirable phone experiences, we need to ensure:

1. **Calls are answered** by a live person, professional message service or answering machine, within an acceptable number of rings (2–3);
2. **Messages are checked** and **responded to** as a matter of urgency;
3. **Callers hear something worthwhile when placed on hold** (if the hold function is used) – ideally, a professional, recorded message via a message-on-hold system, thanking them for their patience and conveying useful information about the business and its services (taking the opportunity to educate, inform and cross-sell).

Ticking these boxes requires a couple of pre-recorded phone messages (an answering message and 'on-hold' message) and the technical infrastructure to deliver them; the combination of which comprises the third essential marketing tool. The infrastructure we need to facilitate automated phone messages can be as simple as a smartphone with a scripted voicemail message, through to a multi-handset KSU (key system unit),

PBX (private branch exchange) or VoIP (voice over internet protocol) telephone system, with a message-on-hold unit if necessary.

A little bit of consideration about the phone experience of our potential customers – and the infrastructure to enhance it – can go a long way to increasing leads, sales and customer satisfaction.

Email Signatures & Canned Responses

An *email signature* is a block of text and images that gets added automatically to the end of our emails. It identifies us and our business – branding our email messages while serving as a digital business card. Among other things, an email signature provides an opportunity to:

- Make your contact details easily accessible;
- Educate recipients about your services, accomplishments and affiliations; and
- Drive traffic to your website and social media pages.

For context, imagine your business has 10 employees, each sending 10 emails a day, 250 days per year. That's 25,000 extra impressions of your logo, contact and service details that wouldn't have otherwise existed, all for no extra work or financial outlay.

An email signature can include:

- A sign-off such as 'Kind regards';
- Your full name and title;
- Your business' logo, slogan and/or subline, embedded as images (ensuring they are not blurry, stretched or otherwise distorted);
- Logo-type images depicting your qualifications, accreditations, memberships or awards;

- Your direct contact details (mobile phone number and email address);
- The business' general contact details (landline number, street and postal address);
- Website address and links to social media profiles (with social media icons embedded as images);
- A concise list of services;
- Announcements about new products or services, client results, etc.

Essentially, an email signature is a free ad. It's an opportunity to enhance the effectiveness of our email communications, requiring a miniscule amount of effort and no extra cost. As such, it's an opportunity that SSB owners are wise not to waste.

Canned email responses are essentially email templates, created in response to common enquiries or questions. Rather than responding to common enquiries from scratch each and every time they are received, the appropriate canned response is selected, personalised and sent. This can save hours of time per week and countless hours per year, while significantly reducing a business' risk of human error and oversight.

Setting up email signatures and canned responses is relatively easy if using a mainstream email platform, but all systems have their quirks. To navigate these, simply search Google or YouTube for instructions specific to your platform of choice (e.g. 'How to set up canned responses in Outlook?'). Failing that, hiring an IT professional – to set up an initial signature and canned response and teach you how to use them – would be well worth it; a small investment for a huge boost in professionalism and efficiency.

Business Cards

Once upon a time, a full suite of professionally printed statio-nery – business cards, letterheads, 'with compliments' slips and envelopes – was essential for SSBs to present a professional image. With advancements in DIY desktop publishing, printing and, more recently, digital communication and file storage, this has all changed. Now, most physical, bulk printed stationery does little more than gather dust... with one exception.

Business cards are as important to SSBs as they ever were. They are fundamental to handshake marketing as well as many other marketing activities – group training, free community facility advertising and point of sale promotion to name a few. They can also serve the dual purpose of a customer service tool – designed with lines on the back to write the date and time of a customer's next appointment.

The quality and professionalism of a business card says a lot about the business it represents, so it's worth investing in a set of decent ones. That said, when starting out in business on a tight budget, a short run of cheap, generic cards can be the wisest option. Investing too much on physical marketing tools too soon, can hold SSB owners back – deterring us from adapting our business model to better position our business for success. Once our business model has stabilised and it's less likely that the design and detail of our business card will change, we can invest more on unique, high-quality design and printing to produce a card that does our business justice.

Before finalising the design of a business card, refer to Chapter 12 of *Secret Service Marketing* – The Truth About Branding – to ensure the basics of your brand are clear and strong, and all essential elements are included.

Promotional Products

Whether it's a pen, mug, stubby holder, keyring, notepad, fridge magnet, power bank or other item of practical use, a branded **promotional product** can be a clever addition to an SSB's marketing arsenal. Although entirely optional, promotional products can be a perfect complement to handshake marketing, point of sale and other face-to-face marketing activities, serving as a semi-permanent bridge between a prospective customer and a business.

Like business cards, promotional products are a physical marketing tool with the capacity to prompt leads and sales into the future. A simple item – such as a branded fridge magnet or mug – can be an excellent way of generating repeat business from first-time or occasional clients, keeping the business top of mind for months or even years. The right promotional product serves as a powerful reminder mechanism, providing constant brand exposure in homes and workplaces. In a welcome way, it infiltrates a prospect's personal environment – boosting brand recognition and recall for far longer than most advertising opportunities.

The distribution of promotional products is a means to support and capitalise on a marketing activity, *not* a marketing activity itself. For SSBs, the use of promotional merchandise is most effective in conjunction with an activity involving human contact and connection – a group training session, for example, which provides the opportunity for positive feelings and memories to be anchored to the gifted product.

All manner of promotional products are available, from branded balloons and beanies to umbrellas and USBs. It's up to us to select one that strikes the right balance between providing visibility for our brand and being valued and appreciated by our customers.

When planning it, the effectiveness of a promotional product strategy can be enhanced by:

1. **Selecting a product relevant to the service you provide** – Promotional products with a strong correlation to the goods or services provided by a business tend to have greater meaning, therefore higher perceived value. Examples include stress balls for a psychology practice, USB drives for an IT support service or vehicle air fresheners for a motor garage.

2. **Giving careful consideration to the product's quality and design** – Promotional products are prized more highly and retained for longer if they're of good quality and adorned with words or images that are clever or symbolic. Beyond a business' logo and basic contact details, a tagline that makes reference to a promotional product's primary function – such as 'Have coffee, will travel' on a transportable coffee cup – can help boost its perceived value.

Whether we're in the financial position to procure promotional merchandise or not, investigating potentially suitable products is a valuable exercise. Not only is it fun to see what's possible, it can open our mind to the possibility of developing a range of products *for sale*.

The research and development of saleable products – whether they're branded usables (drink bottles and backpacks for a gym, or teapots and mugs for a café), consumables (nutritional supplements or packs of specialty tea) or information products (introduced in Chapter 4) – is something every entrepreneurial SSB owner should explore, or at least entertain. It can spark the discovery of a game-changing approach to market and associated revenue stream, leading to the development of a more scalable, sustainable business model. It's worth noting, however, that – to be appealing enough for customers to pay money for – a product must be relevant to the service provided, high enough quality that it won't undermine the business' reputation and more subtly branded than products developed to give away for free.

———————

Strong Tools Rule

If you take one thing away from this book, let it be the concept of the Secret Service Six. The strength of our marketing tools goes a long way to determining the success of the marketing activities we pursue. With a website that applies the Secret Service Website Formula, a well-planned sales kit, a professional email signature, an appropriate suite of automated phone messages and canned email responses, decent business cards and, optionally, a promotional product or two, our marketing arsenal is exponentially stronger. That means the marketing activities we engage in have the capacity to work better than they otherwise would. We can generate more leads and sales from them with less input, effort and risk… the ultimate no-brainer, really.

CHAPTER 7.

MARKETING DECISIONS MADE EASIER

*** WARNING! DETAIL AHEAD ***
This chapter contains detailed instructions that
may be overwhelming at first. If you get bogged
down in it, switch to skim reading and return
to each section as it becomes applicable.

As you familiarise yourself with the marketing tools and activities at your disposal, another can of worms opens up. 'How many activities does my business need? Which activities should I try first? Should I focus on free opportunities or skip straight to paid advertising? Is it better to prioritise online or offline marketing?' and more. So, let's set a few things straight.

The optimum number and type of marketing activities varies from one SSB to another. There's no right or wrong quantity or combination. I've had many trade service clients who, upon overhauling their website with the Lead Machine Blueprints supplied in *The Secret Service Website Formula*, required next to no additional marketing activity to sustain their business. Within a matter of weeks, leads started rolling in. This is possible when a business is generating enough exposure organically – from its physical presence in the community and pre-existing presence in search engines – that a new website (a strategically crafted Lead Machine) is all it takes to capitalise on it. The new site simply equips the business to make the most of traffic that was already there.

Other SSBs need to be more active in pursuing new customers because the market they exist in is too competitive for awareness to be generated organically. When lots of similar businesses are vying for attention in a given market, those that aren't actively pursuing it by investing in marketing activity get lost in the crowd. The attention and resultant traffic, leads and sales go to the businesses that *do* make that investment.

There's no magic formula to determine an optimal combination of marketing activities, but there is a formula to help find it quicker.

The Secret Service Kick-Start Code

Whether you're starting an SSB or overhauling an existing one as a novice Secret Service Marketer, the code to remember to help prioritise, select and budget for marketing tools and activities is *5–5–5*. This stands for:

5 Marketing tools (the first five of the Secret Service Six, introduced in Chapter 6)

- ▪ A Lead Machine (website geared to drive leads)
- ▪ A sales kit

- Automated phone messages
- Email signatures and canned responses
- Business cards

5 Survival marketing activities

- Networking
- Manual sales prospecting
- Word of mouth
- Telemarketing – inbound
- Point of sale promotion – personal selling

5 No-brainer marketing activities (selected from the 12 presented in Chapter 3)

- Alliance building
- Online directories – free listings
- Comparator websites
- Online review management
- Public relations management
- Search engine optimisation – DIY
- Point of sale promotion – promotional paraphernalia
- Asset advertising
- Community facility advertising – free or low cost
- Resident distribution advertising – DIY
- Local markets
- Celebrity appeal marketing

This suite of 5 tools and 10 activities is a time and cost effective combination and an ideal starting point for any SSB. Implementing them might take a few months or more, but heading in the right direction is what counts; making decisions and allocating resources in a business' best interest. The Kick-Start Code is a framework to guide these early decisions – preventing bright, shiny objects (in the form of high-risk marketing opportunities) from throwing the business off course.

Getting the first **5** (the essential marketing tools) in place as soon as possible is strongly recommended, as these are key to capitalising on low-risk marketing activities. With strong tools in place, a business can start small, simple and inexpensive – with an arsenal of survival and no-brainer activities – then gradually add cheap but challenging and upper end activities if needed. Implementing free, low-cost and low-input activities before expensive or time-consuming ones is wise because – if they prove effective enough to sustain the business (which *is* possible) – it can save an exorbitant amount of time, money and marketing frustration down the track. It may even save the business itself.

Beyond the 15 initial tools and activities, everything else is optional: promotional products (the sixth tool), the seven remaining no-brainers, plus all cheap but challenging and upper end activities – listed for quick reference below:

Cheap but challenging activities (optional)

- Group training
- Content marketing
- Information products
- Social media activity
- Telemarketing – outbound
- Email marketing
- Mobile marketing
- Snail mail marketing
- Viral marketing
- Street marketing – low cost

Upper end activities (optional)

- Expos and trade shows
- Online directories – paid listings
- Group buying (daily deal) website campaigns
- Search engine optimisation – outsourced
- Search engine advertising
- Social media advertising
- Community facility advertising – paid
- Resident distribution advertising – paid
- Street marketing – high cost
- Mainstream media advertising

Marketing should be a fun business function, not torture. If a cheap but challenging or upper end activity doesn't feel right – the effort or expense of it causing you to feel a sense of heaviness, drudgery or financial overwhelm – it's not the right fit, and that's okay. Not all activities are a good fit for every SSB owner. The quicker we acknowledge them, let them go, and move on to the other spokes of the Marketing Wheel, guilt-free, the faster we'll reach our business goals.

Assessing the fit of a cheap but challenging activity relies heavily on gut feel. It's a matter of gauging what's involved – through online research, courses, workshops and most valuably, discussions with other SSB owners who undertake the activity – then reflecting on your capacity to undertake and commit to it yourself. While cheap but challenging activities (such as DIY SEO or social media activity) don't cost much money, they do take time, energy and a willingness to learn and grow. If we're not honest with ourselves about what an activity involves and what we're prepared to put into it, we're unlikely to get much out of it. But if we do our groundwork, reflect honestly on the logistics of the activity and still feel enthusiastic about it, that's all the evidence needed to justify moving forward.

Assessing the fit of expensive marketing activities – particularly mainstream media advertising and other upper end opportunities – requires a more comprehensive, fact-based analysis, due to the money and risk involved. If a cheap but challenging activity falls flat, it's unlikely to break the bank. If an upper end activity falls flat, it's a whole other story; one that can send a struggling SSB into a tailspin. To avoid this, a methodical, non-emotional approach to the consideration of paid marketing opportunities is needed, as outlined below.

Assessing the Fit & Feasibility of a Paid Marketing Activity

Step 1. Look for long-term benefits

Before doing any in-depth analysis, one of the most important things to consider about a paid marketing activity is whether it could have any residual benefits. With some paid activities, this is par for the course. Outsourced SEO, for example, aims to boost organic website traffic on an ongoing basis – the benefits of which can continue to be seen, long after an SEO contract ends. Asset advertising is another prime example, with premises and vehicle signage providing local exposure for years or even decades after installation. However, these are the exceptions.

Most paid marketing opportunities provide short-term exposure, therefore short-term results. If we stop paying, our ads stop displaying. And if our ads stop displaying, our ability to reach potential customers grinds to a halt. While paid ads can provide a period of residual benefit due to them being retained in the memory bank of the odd service seeker, it's small – certainly not enough to generate an ongoing flow of leads. That's not to say that upper end activities without long-term benefits are bad – they just need to be used with caution.

In most cases, if an activity's cost is high and its benefits are expected to be short-lived, dipping a toe in the water with one or two isolated ads will do nothing but deplete your bank account. Thinking and budgeting bigger than a one-off ad is essential, because upper end marketing activities take time to ramp up to their full potential. A TV viewer needs several views of a commercial over a period of time to process the information, let alone consider taking action. One or two ads doesn't allow for this. Instead, a suitably comprehensive and impactful *campaign* is required – considered in terms of ad substance, frequency and duration.

If you can't afford to advertise constantly or at regular intervals (depending on the medium) for a sustained period of time, without deriving any additional sales from it, then the activity will be a long shot. And if your livelihood is at stake, it's just not worth the risk.

Step 2. Interrogate the sales rep

When considering any marketing opportunity with a hefty price tag, asking the right questions is key to making an informed decision.

Like most of us, sales representatives for advertising and other marketing opportunities only promote the details, facts and statistics that support their cause – those that will make their prospects more likely to sign on the dotted line. Any information that doesn't support their cause will remain buried, unless we dig it up. This is done by asking questions geared to determine the real relevance of the advertising opportunity to us and our target market. Digging for the details upfront is much easier than trying to dig our way out of an airtight contract six months down the track, having learned the hard way that the marketing opportunity wasn't a good fit.

Beyond the obvious questions regarding what's involved and how much it will cost, questions to ask sales reps selling *offline* opportunities, such as TV, radio or magazine advertising, include:

- 'What is the distribution area (geographic reach) of the channel/publication?' With this information, you can deduce if the location of viewers/readers aligns with the region you service, or if you would be paying to advertise to people located outside your service area.
- 'How many people in my service area actively view/ listen to/read your channel/publication?' and 'How is this measured?'
- 'Who are these viewers/listeners/readers in terms of age, gender, interest, etc (in other words, what are the demographics of the channel/publication's audience) and do these demographics align with my business' target market?'
- 'What businesses similar to mine – in terms of type, size and location – have undertaken this marketing activity recently and what were their results?'

For *online* advertising opportunities, such as paid directory listings, a list of questions is provided on page 108.

It's not enough to rely on a sales rep's verbal estimations or best guesses in response to these questions. If you don't see documented facts or examples as proof, the responses can't be relied upon. Remember that ad sales reps are paid to promote and sell their one option. This makes them 100% biassed. To cut through this bias and have the capacity to make an informed decision, a healthy sense of scepticism is essential, as is the courage to cross-examine any verbal claims.

Step 3. Crunch the numbers

If, after steps 1 and 2, the opportunity still seems promising, it's time to consider its financial feasibility.

1. **Identify, list and add up all possible costs** – The total cost of an upper end activity consists not only of the base fees or charges (the ad rate of a TV commercial or the stand hire fee at an expo) but all costs required to execute it effectively.

   A critical determinant of the success of any marketing activity is the content of the ad or event materials. This can include copywriting or scriptwriting, design, photography and/or videography. To give an activity the best possible chance, these creative costs must be budgeted for, along with any logistical and operational outlays.

   The total cost of participating in an expo, for example, may include:
   - Stand hire fee;
   - Equipment and decor hire;
   - Design, copywriting and printing of sales/ promotional materials and signage;
   - Transportation;
   - Staffing;
   - Sales lost while the business is closed to attend the event;
   - And more.

2. **Determine the conversion you want the activity to inspire** – Identifying a specific action you'd like prospects to take as a result of the marketing activity is paramount, whether it's purchasing a particular package, booking a certain service, completing an enquiry form or engaging in an on-the-spot, face-to-face transaction at your premises or expo stand. A clear conversion action is key to making a calculated decision about the feasibility of an upper end activity, via a break even analysis (step 4). If you decide to proceed, it's also key to developing an appealing offer and call-to-action, and evaluating the effectiveness of the activity afterwards.

3. **Work out what a conversion is worth** – Once you know the conversion action you want the proposed activity to encourage, work out how much a single conversion would be worth to your business. Sometimes, this figure is easy to find – it's the *selling price* of a focus product or package decided upon in step 2. However, if this product has an attributable production cost (known as *cost of sales*, *cost of goods sold* or *COGS*), it needs to be taken into account – deducting it from the selling price to reveal the ***gross profit*** of a conversion. Using gross profit to assess an activity's feasibility (rather than a product's selling price) is preferable, as it provides a more accurate indication of the minimum number of sales required from the activity to break even.

   For some SSBs, the break even point can be more accurately calculated by substituting gross profit for another figure. Businesses that provide an ongoing service to individual clients, such as bookkeepers or fitness instructors, may be best to use a figure that represents the *average lifetime value of a customer (CLV)*, while businesses with a longer, more involved sales process, such as web designers or builders, can be better off using a figure that represents the *average value of a lead* – taking into account the business' sales conversion rate (the percentage of leads successfully converted into sales). Determine a figure that provides the most accurate representation of the value of a single conversion to your business before proceeding to the next step.

4. **Calculate the break even point of the activity** – This is done by dividing the total cost of the marketing activity (from step 1), by the conversion value (step 3). The result indicates how many conversions (e.g. sales or bookings) will need to be generated from the activity for it to prove financially viable.

Total cost of the marketing activity / Single *conversion value* = Number of *conversions required to break even*

Example: Luigi's Restaurant
Luigi is considering participating in a high-end wedding expo to promote his restaurant as a function venue.
- Total cost of the expo – $8,000
- Selling price of the average wedding function – $150 per head x 50pax = $7500
- Direct cost to produce/service the average wedding function – $95 per head x 50pax = $4750

> To break even, the number of wedding function bookings Luigi would need to generate from the expo is calculated as follows:
>
> **Total cost** of the marketing activity / Single **conversion value** = Number of **conversions required to break even**
>
> $8000 / ($7500 − $4750)
>
>   = $8000 / $2750
>
>   = 2.9
>
>   = 3 wedding functions (rounded up to a whole number) and $22,500 (3 x $7500) in wedding function sales

The assessment of a paid marketing opportunity doesn't stop there though. Just because the break even point seems reasonable, there's no guarantee the required conversions will come to fruition. It's a risk. But we can get a clearer idea of the extent of that risk by adding one last step to the assessment process...

Step 4. Get the word on the street

As mentioned earlier, sales representatives for marketing activities are biassed. Whether they're from a search engine marketing agency, an online directory, a television network or the local paper, they'll claim their system, strategy or solution is the best. After all, that's their job. Despite how much they may genuinely believe in their product, they can't be relied upon to provide objective advice, nor sell us the exact marketing solution we need. They are paid to present a narrow, rosy view of the options. That's not to say sales reps aren't reliable and trustworthy people, just that they have a narrow field of vision relative to the options and opportunities available. So, to make a truly informed decision, we must be prepared to bypass them – going around them to get the lowdown on the opportunity they're offering.

Bypassing the sales rep means seeking the honest insights of business owners who have undertaken the activity. This is done by reaching out to businesses that currently advertise via the channel, publication or platform under consideration – or have done so in the recent past – to get independent, unsolicited feedback. A two-minute phone conversation with a current or past advertiser can be incredibly enlightening – helping to evaluate the real life effectiveness of the activity and get a clearer indication as to whether it's worth the investment.

Contacting past/present advertisers can be done in three steps:

1. **Identify advertisers/exhibitors** – The easiest way to identify businesses who use or have used a particular activity is to ask the sales rep (if applicable) for business names, with a view to making contact with them. Note, however, that going about it this way, you risk hearing all the good stories and none of the bad.

   The alternative is to undertake your own independent enquiry. This involves accessing the channel/publication/platform under consideration for a period of time (be it a paid online directory such as the Yellow Pages, classified ads for trade services in the local paper, or free-to-air TV) to manually identify current and recent SSB advertisers. Identifying past exhibitors of an expo or trade show can be more challenging, but it's often possible to find an old brochure or list of exhibitors via a quick online search.

2. **Select relevant advertisers/exhibitors** – Equipped with a list of past/present advertisers, narrow it down to one or two to contact. An ideal business to reach out to will be similar to yours in size and scope, but not in direct competition with you – whether they service a neighbouring region or have a different field of specialisation. This point of difference is important as it will help the owner perceive you as a comrade, not a threat, and feel comfortable divulging their opinion and results. If many businesses fit the bill, select those advertising at the ad level, rate or time-slot you are considering.

3. **Make the call/s** – This is where it gets interesting. Phone the business owner and explain the situation – who you are, where you're from (including the reason your business is different to theirs to mitigate any perceived threat) and that you're considering advertising/exhibiting via the channel/publication/platform they do or did, but want to make sure you're making an informed decision. If this is well received, go on to ask if they'd mind sharing their experience with you – if they had much luck with the activity, whether they generated many quality leads from it and if they would undertake the activity again. If the activity worked for them and the phone call is going particularly well, ask if there is anything they've discovered that works better for them, in terms of ad size, placement, scheduling, etc. To wrap things up, thank them profusely for their time and insights.

As a side note, if you find the prospect of making phone calls like this stressful, refer to Chapter 6 of *Secret Service Marketing* for advice on overcoming phone phobia.

As much as an upper end marketing activity may seem like a good opportunity and feasible in theory, there's nothing as valuable as an honest, upfront conversation with someone who's walked the path you're seeking to tread. Not only is contacting previous advertisers/exhibitors key to evaluating if the break even point you've calculated is realistic, it can expose subtle flaws and failings of the activity which you'd otherwise be left to discover the hard way... by flushing thousands of dollars down the drain.

Navigating the Numbers

Although the process of assessing a paid marketing activity may sound time-consuming, it doesn't need to take long. The most challenging parts tend to be points 2 and 3 of step 3: determining the conversion you want to encourage and calculating the value of that conversion to your business. This can be a particularly daunting task for those with a weak business model, or a variable or post-op pricing strategy who win work by quoting on custom jobs or projects.[10]

For SSB owners with a weak business model, embarking on an expensive marketing activity can be a monumental, potentially fatal mistake. If experiencing unpredictable or inconsistent business performance, poor conversion rates, or feelings of uncertainty or distress about your business' ability to compete and survive, marketing activity – at any price – is *not* the answer. The solution lies in the creation of a strong, sustainable business model (a process for which can be found in Part 3 of *Secret Service Marketing* – Survival of the Fittest) and an equally strong set of marketing tools. Only when we have confidence in our business model and marketing tools should we consider embarking on an upper end marketing activity. Any sooner than that can spell disaster for an already flailing SSB.

For those with a business model that encompasses post-op pricing, deciding on and valuing the conversion we want a marketing activity to generate can present a real challenge; careful consideration can quickly turn into analysis paralysis. It's important to remember that giving the assessment process a go – using averages or approximations where necessary – will always be better than making a flippant decision based on a sales pitch alone. Any attempt is better than no attempt.

Assessing an Activity's Performance

The assessment of a marketing activity doesn't stop with a decision to go ahead with it. No matter what activity we embark upon, tracking and assessing its performance – in terms of traffic, views, leads, sales or other applicable indicators – is essential. Without monitoring, recording and analysing the results an activity generates, we'll be evaluating its performance by assumption alone. We won't know for certain if it's working and to what extent, or have any quantitative basis for repeating the activity in future. In the case of activities such as search engine advertising, which give us the ability to adjust our approach mid-campaign, we'll also miss the opportunity to test, measure and refine our ads, causing us to waste money when we could be making more.

How we track performance depends on the activity. Most online marketing activities offer a dashboard of information and the ability to drill down into automatically recorded data to obtain deeper insights. This can make tracking easier and more accurate than for offline activities, but also more overwhelming.

While an intricate dashboard of information can provide fascinating insights, it's equally fascinating – and arguably more important – to take a step back and assess the activity in terms of simple ***return on investment (ROI).***

Marketing ROI (Return on Investment)

Calculating the ROI of a marketing activity helps us put the results it generates into context. It enables us to compare its performance with that of other activities – as well as the results achieved by other businesses – to determine what warrants a place in our business' marketing arsenal and what doesn't.

To calculate the simple ROI of a marketing activity, we need two figures – the *investment* (cost of the activity) and the *return* (sales generated by the activity), for a given period of time. The following formula is then applied:

$$\text{Simple ROI} = \frac{(\text{Return or Sales Growth} - \text{Investment})}{\text{Investment}}$$

Return: the total sales or increase in sales generated by the marketing activity.
Investment: the total spent on the marketing activity during that same period.

The *investment* or cost of an activity is determined in the same way as in step 3.1 of the viability assessment but using *actual* expenditure in place of estimates. The *return* or sales generated by an activity can be a little harder to nail down. The three most practical ways to track the return generated by an activity are outlined below.

1. **Manual tracking** – For businesses with a relatively low number of customers – those providing design, construction, finance or cleaning services, for example – simply asking new customers how they heard about your business, then recording the response and associated sale amount, can be an effective form of tracking. Whether it's asked in person during the sales process or via a 'How did you hear about us?' drop-down box in your website's enquiry form (with options for 'Local newspaper', 'Google search', 'Shop-a-Docket' or whatever activities are in use), this one little question can be enough to expose the activities that are working and those that aren't. As long as the question is asked consistently and your customers' responses are recorded accurately, it can be all that's needed to track the effectiveness of your marketing activities.

2. **Calculating the sales growth (change in revenue)** – For businesses with a high number of customers, such as a café, a more practical way to measure the return generated from a marketing activity is to take the average revenue for the period prior to the ad campaign (or during the same period in previous years) and use it as a base to calculate the change in revenue in the campaign period. Although this is a less accurate approach, it can be enough to provide an insight into the impact of an activity. If using this method, it's a good idea to introduce one new marketing activity at a time, so the correlation between each activity and ROI is as clear as possible.

3. **Creating a unique offer for each activity** – A third way to track the results of a marketing activity is to incentivise the

call-to-action with a coupon or special offer that's unique to that particular activity, then track coupon redemption or offer uptake. No matter the volume of customers or number of advertising campaigns running at any one time, this method of tracking is quite simple and reliable. However, because it requires a strong promotional offer, it can have an adverse effect on gross profit, which needs to be taken into consideration.

Once the return generated by a marketing activity has been tracked, the return on investment can be calculated using the simple ROI formula.

Example ROI calculation

An ad campaign generates $5000 of extra sales. The ads cost $1200.

Simple ROI = (Return or Sales Growth – Investment) / Investment

= ($5000 – $1200) / $1200

= $3800 / $1200

= 317% ROI or **3:1** when expressed as a ratio

Although this looks like a great result, it may not be. That's because the simple ROI formula doesn't take COGS (the cost of goods sold) into consideration. Not all of the return is profit – it encompasses the direct costs of producing the product or service. Without taking COGS into account, it's easy to think a marketing activity has reaped a reasonable return, when it's actually bleeding the business dry.

For this reason, a decent ROI is typically around 5:1. At that, a marketing activity is usually contributing more to a business than it's costing and would probably be worth continuing or repeating. However, it's up to us to know and understand our business' gross profit margins and take them into account when calculating ROI, so we know what result indicates that an activity has been effective and can draw on it as a benchmark moving forward.

The Hustle and Flow of Modern Marketing

Like children, businesses are unique entities with a blend of characteristics, quirks and considerations like no other – and they don't come with instruction manuals. The combination of marketing activities that works for one business won't necessarily work for the next. As SSB owners, it's our job to figure out what combination works for our particular business. This takes time, persistence and a willingness to navigate the *hustle* and *flow* of modern marketing – aka *manual* and *automated* marketing.

Manual marketing strategies are tools and activities reliant on our physical presence or involvement. They include handshake marketing, training workshops, social media activity, email marketing, telemarketing, blogging, public relations initiatives and more… anything that requires us to prepare, create content and/or exert physical effort on an ongoing basis.

Automated marketing strategies are less reliant on us. They can take a bit of work to set up and maintain but, for the most part, they are hands-off. A Lead Machine and healthy Google Business Profile (complete with 5-star reviews), active alliances and tried-and-tested advertising campaigns are prime examples. Once they're set up and refined, they can provide a steady drip-feed of leads and sales to an SSB, like an automatic irrigation system waters a garden without having to pick up a hose. But, just as an irrigation system doesn't teach us to read and respond to the nuances of our garden, automated marketing doesn't teach us to read and respond to the nuances of our business environment. Only the hard yards of manual marketing can do that.

Manual marketing is the *hustle* required to become a successful SSB owner. It's how we earn our stripes. It's knocking on doors, cold calling strangers, pounding the pavement, stepping outside our social comfort zone in the quest for leads, facing fears of rejection, judgement and public speaking, and putting the cash flow needs of our business baby ahead of our own comforts and insecurities. The hustle is hard, but it has to be... it's the right of passage to sustainable business success.

As a business matures, it's possible to start relying less on hustle and more on the flow of an automated marketing arsenal. As long as you're committed to continual improvement – striving to adapt, innovate, evolve and grow – the number of leads that flow in organically, will increase. There will always be times you have to hustle, but by that stage you're a hustle master, so familiar with pushing outside your comfort zone for the good of your business that it no longer feels hard. It becomes a welcome challenge.

No one can tell you the exact combination of marketing activities that will fuel the growth and success of your business but, hopefully, this book serves as a handy reference point, so you know what you've got in your arsenal at any given time and where to start to make the biggest bang.

A FINAL WORD

THE SERVICE REVOLUTION

As I write this, the world is at the tail-end of the COVID-19 pandemic; regaining some semblance of normality after a tumultuous, societal roller coaster ride.

Beyond those who've endured the worst of the virus as a sufferer, carer or loved one, small skill-or-service businesses have been some of the hardest hit. Comprising around 78% of the business population[11] and employing a whopping 75–85% of the workforce,[12] the SSB community is the economic ground zero of this pandemic. With millions forced to operate in a restricted capacity or close their doors completely, the collateral damage – the toll taken on individuals, families, communities and the world at large – is immeasurable.

It was while contemplating the gravity of this at my dining room table (making the most of a lockdown to get an extra chapter over the line) that it became clear why the *Secret Service Business Series* has come to be.

Whispers of a **Service Revolution** have been heard on the wind for decades now. Many corporate commentators have interpreted this as a 'customer service revolution' in which big businesses will need to overhaul their customer offerings and experiences to meet ever-rising consumer expectations, and maintain their precious economies of scale.

I have a different view.

As it stands, we are in the **Fourth Industrial Revolution (4IR)**. The original **Industrial Revolution** saw the introduction of mechanisation, steam and water power. The **Second Industrial Revolution (2IR)** brought us mass production and electricity. The **Third (3IR)** introduced electronic and IT systems, automation, the internet and communication technologies. This swiftly led to the **4IR**, with the emergence of smart technologies, cyber physical systems, virtual reality and artificial intelligence.

Here, amid the radical change of the 4IR, we are hitting a wall – not in terms of our intellectual or technological capabilities, but in terms of ethics. As Marc Benioff (co-CEO of Salesforce) observed so eloquently, we've reached 'a crisis of trust in technology' and something's got to give.[13]

The human race is at an ethical crossroads and COVID-19 has brought the decision to turn left or right to a head. We can forge ahead with the 4IR, no matter the cost to the planet or its people, paving the way to a terrifying reality **(5IR)** in which artificial intelligence supersedes human consciousness. Or, we can close the book on the Industrial Revolution, bringing the best from it (sanitation, renewable energy, medical advancements and smart technologies for example) and leaving the worst (authoritarianism, oil tankers, coal mines, sweatshops, pollution, Big Food, Big Pharma and the like) to embark on a bold new era; one in which the wellbeing of our planet and its people come above all else, through service to the world and each other.

It's my belief that a Service Revolution – in various stages, like the Industrial Revolution before it – will be underpinned by a major energetic shift, resulting from the reevaluation of priorities brought about by COVID-19 (and subsequent global shake-ups, if we don't take the hint and act now).

While it's impossible to predict exactly how the Service Revolution will play out, it's likely to be characterised by:

1. Rapid income growth, job creation, gender equality and poverty reduction led by services (as India has proved possible);[14]

2. A more conscious approach to product creation and consumption;

3. Innovation grounded by integrity and sustainability;

4. Compassionate leadership (modelled extensively by women);

5. A realisation of the societal and monetary benefits of prioritising and nurturing the physical, spiritual and mental wellbeing of constituents, employees and consumers by governments and corporate bodies;

6. A shift in the balance of power in the business world, from big business to small – stemming from: 1) SSB owners embracing the power of being small and marketing themselves accordingly, and 2) a change in consumer priorities and spending habits, as more of us wake up to the fact that money and material goods do not equate to happiness.

In a nutshell, the Service Revolution will be characterised by collectivism, compassion, conscious creation and consumption, and the enhancement and empowerment of the individual, for the greater good.

As the pandemic has highlighted for so many of us, it's the small freedoms and simple comforts of heart and home that matter. Physical and mental health. Quality time and experiences with family and friends. A safe, functional home that brings us peace and respite. Self improvement, introspection and education. Respect and appreciation for the services of others. Finding a way to be of service ourselves. The world is awakening to what brings true happiness, and mass consumption driven by manipulative marketing messages is not it.

As SSB owners, we are not only on the precipice of the Service Revolution, we are a driving force behind it. By becoming Secret Service Marketers, we have the capacity to lead the charge – acknowledging our soul's yearning to be of service and connecting it with the principles and practicalities of surviving in the modern world.

So take the *Secret Service Business Series* and run with it. You have all you need to recover from the pandemic and build a stronger, more satisfying business. And know that in doing so, you are contributing to the most critical gear-change in human history – out of the industrial age and into an age of service. Together, we just might change the world... all while living with integrity and authenticity, providing for our families, supporting our communities and creating a life we love.

YOUR MICRO MISSION

Congratulations! You finished *The Modern Marketing Arsenal* – the third and final book in the *Secret Service Business Series*.

To help the Secret Service approach gain momentum, there are a few things you can do:

1. **Share the love** – Post a short review of this book (complete with a photo or two) on your social media platform of choice, or wherever you bought it online. This is one of the best ways to help others discover the series for themselves.
2. **Lend, gift or recommend** the book to a struggling SSB owner, designer or content creator.
3. **Look local** – Ask your community bookshop or library to stock the Secret Service Business Series, if they don't already.
4. **Loop yourself in** – Join the Secret Service revolution by subscribing to occasional updates via *www.secretservice.biz* (scan the code and sign up now).

Thank you for supporting the *Secret Service Business Series*. I wish you all the best in putting what you've learned into practice.

Laura de Lacy
Author & Secret Service Marketer

ACKNOWLEDGEMENTS

Producing the Secret Service Business Series was a mission made possible by many. A huge thank you to Isabelle Russell, Gianna Grbich and Tatsiana Teush for your dedication and expertise; David, Jessica and Keely at Green Hill Publishing for your patience and professionalism; Nett Hulse, Natasha Pintaric, Gianna, Michelle Ridland, Jason Lehman and Thomas Le Coz for your support and valued contributions over the years; the small business owners I've had the privilege to work with – each one instrumental in nutting out the Secret Service approach; Graham McGuiggan; Peter Daniels and Brett McFall for your trust and tutelage; Gordon Kay for proving that integrity and generosity **do** belong in business (when I was starting to doubt it); Brad, Corinne and Caro for your strength and inspiration, in life and from above; Billy for believing in me before I was ready to; Ellie and Evie for being our village; Lovell and Jacqui (my earth angels) for paying it forward; the de Lacy and Braithwaite clans – my family and best mates; And last but not least, William Devlin... 'I may have given you life, but you gave me mine'.

INDEX

ENDNOTES

1   The Busy/Slow Cycle is a common SSB phenomena – a rhythm of business in which sales fluctuate over time. It is explained in detail in Chapter 2 of *Secret Service Marketing*, along with the insights required to overcome it.

2   A performance persona is the most personable and attentive version of an individual (business owner or staff member), existing to anticipate and fulfil the needs of their customers with passion and purpose – explained in detail in Chapter 5 of *Secret Service Marketing*.

3   Tripadvisor is a global comparator site for accommodation providers, restaurants and tourist attractions.

4   Refer to Chapter 20 of *The Secret Service Website Formula* for details.

5   Australian Competition and Consumer Commission – Door-to-door and telemarketing sales www.accc.gov.au/business/advertising-promoting-your-business/door-to-door-telemarketing-sales

6   Content Marketing Institute (2021), *What exactly is Content Marketing*, www.contentmarketinginstitute.com/getting-started

7   Forleo, M (22 Feb 2017), *Cheryl Strayed on How To Become a Writer, The Power of Art and More*, MarieTV www.youtube.com/watch?v=oINfXbPsVqM

8   BrightEdge Research (May 2019), *Organic Search Improves Ability to Map to Consumer Intent: Organic Channel Share Expands to 53.3% of Traffic*, p4 https://videos.brightedge.com/research-report/BrightEdge_ChannelReport2019_FINAL.pdf

9   Lant, J (1995), *Money Making Marketing: Finding the People Who Need What You're Selling and Making Sure They Buy It*, Jeffrey Lant Assocs

10 Pricing strategies are explained in Chapter 10 of *Secret Service Marketing* – The Price is Right... or is it?

11 Estimate calculated from: Australian Bureau of Statistics (2022), *Counts of Australian Businesses, including Entries & Exits, July 2018 – June 2022*, Data Cube 1, Tables 1 & 13a

12 House of Representatives Standing Committee EFPA (2007), Services Export Report – *Servicing Our Future*, Chapter 2 – Overview of Australia's Services Sector, Sections 2.56 & 2.63 https://www.aph.gov.au/parliamentary_business/committees/house_of_representatives_committees?url=efpa/services/report.htm

13 Lauchlan S (January 2019), *The Fifth Industrial Revolution is coming – and it's about trust, values and saving the planet*, Diginomica www.diginomica.com/the-fifth-industrial-revolution-is-coming-and-its-about-trust-values-and-saving-the-planet

14 Ghani E & Kharas H (May 2010), *The Service Revolution*, The World Bank – Economic Premise, Number 14

www.ingramcontent.com/pod-product-compliance
Lightning Source LLC
Chambersburg PA
CBHW030538210326
41597CB00014B/1200